Last Stand at Zandvoorde 1914

To Trevor

Mike McBride

Dedicated to:

Major General Gerald Cavendish Grosvenor
6th Duke of Westminster
KG CB CVO OBE TD CD DL
Grandson of Captain Lord Hugh William Grosvenor

Last Stand at Zandvoorde 1914

Lord Hugh Grosvenor's Noble Sacrifice

Mike McBride

Pen & Sword
MILITARY

First published in Great Britain in 2016 by
Pen & Sword Military
an imprint of
Pen & Sword Books Ltd
47 Church Street
Barnsley
South Yorkshire
S70 2AS

ISBN 978 1 47389 157 9

A CIP catalogue record for this book is available from the British
Library

Typeset in Ehrhardt by
Mac Style Ltd, Bridlington, East Yorkshire
Printed and bound in the UK by CPI Group (UK) Ltd,
Croydon, CRO 4YY

Pen & Sword Books Ltd incorporates the imprints of Pen & Sword
Archaeology, Atlas, Aviation, Battleground, Discovery, Family
History, History, Maritime, Military, Naval, Politics, Railways, Select,
Transport, True Crime, and Fiction, Frontline Books, Leo Cooper,
Praetorian Press, Seaforth Publishing and Wharncliffe.

For a complete list of Pen & Sword titles please contact
PEN & SWORD BOOKS LIMITED
47 Church Street, Barnsley, South Yorkshire, S70 2AS, England
E-mail: enquiries@pen-and-sword.co.uk
Website: www.pen-and-sword.co.uk

Contents

Grosvenor Family Tree 1914

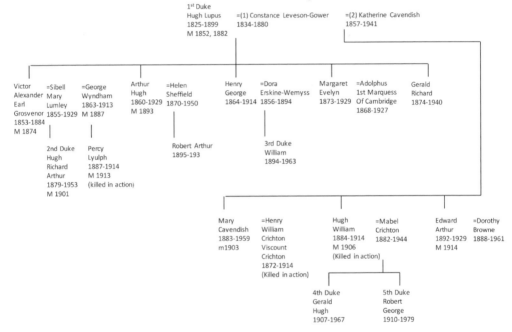

1st Duke
Hugh Lupus   =(1) Constance Leveson-Gower   =(2) Katherine Cavendish
1825-1899   1834-1880   1857-1941
M 1852, 1882

Victor   =Sibell   =George   Arthur   =Helen   Henry   =Dora   Margaret   =Adolphus   Gerald
Alexander   Mary   Wyndham   Hugh   Sheffield   George   Erskine-Wemyss Evelyn   1st Marquess   Richard
Earl   Lumley   1863-1913   1860-1929   1870-1950   1864-1914   1856-1894   1873-1929   Of Cambridge   1874-1940
Grosvenor   1855-1929   M 1887   M 1893   1868-1927
1853-1884
M 1874

                2nd Duke   Percy   Robert Arthur   3rd Duke
                Hugh   Lyulph   1895-193   William
                Richard   1887-1914   1894-1963
                Arthur   M 1913
                1879-1953   (killed in action)
                M 1901

                            Mary   =Henry   Hugh   =Mabel   Edward   =Dorothy
                            Cavendish   William   William   Crichton   Arthur   Browne
                            1883-1959   Crichton   1884-1914   1882-1944   1892-1929   1888-1961
                            m1903   Viscount   M 1906   M 1914
                                        Crichton   (Killed in action)
                                        1872-1914
                                        (Killed in action)

                                        4th Duke   5th Duke
                                        Gerald   Robert
                                        Hugh   George
                                        1907-1967   1910-1979

This abbreviated family tree shows a selection of the relatives of the 1st Duke
of Westminster connected with the telling of *Last Stand at Zandvoorde*

Prologue

Zandvoorde, Ypres, Belgium, October 1914 – The situation could hardly have been any worse. Battle-weary British soldiers were holding onto the frontline by their fingertips. The muddy ridge they were clinging on to just outside Ypres was vital. If the German Army could smash their way through the remnants of the British line they could march on to the Channel ports and knock Britain out of the War. Manning a section of the forward most trenches to thwart the enemy were about a hundred men of the Household Cavalry led by Captain Lord Hugh William Grosvenor.

The Official History described the predicament:

> 'The line that stood between the British Empire and ruin was composed of tired haggard and unshaven men, many in uniforms that were little more than rags.'

When the Germans attacked Lord Hugh and his Squadron disappeared.

> 'Not one officer or man, not a button or a rifle, nothing of that Squadron has ever been seen or heard of to this day. No graves were ever discovered. No capture was ever reported. It was as though they had never been.'

Preface

Nearly a million British and Empire soldiers fought and died in the First World War. Why then should attention be focused on just one man – Captain Lord Hugh William Grosvenor?

During the three short weeks in which Lord Hugh fought in the Belgian region of Flanders he was a witness to massive changes in warfare such as the practical destruction of the best of Britain's regular army, the British Expeditionary Force or BEF. He also saw the end of centuries of massed cavalry operations and the chivalric era that stretched back to armoured knights on horseback.

Additionally, Lord Hugh was to experience advances in military hardware such as the aeroplane, the armoured fighting vehicle, the machine-gun and, tragically, the devastating effect of modern artillery.

The British Army which eventually won victory in 1918 was fundamentally different in training, organization, equipment and tactics from the army Lord Hugh knew. The enhancements in military science were won through the hard lessons of combat experience. The eventual allied success was built on the sacrifices of Lord Hugh and his comrades.

A century after Lord Hugh's death his experience provides a valuable insight into the First World War and a gateway for a new generation to understand the harsh reality of war.

Through official records, eye witness accounts and, especially, previously unpublished letters home from Lord Hugh one can get some appreciation of the chaotic and desperate actions at a critical phase of the First World War.

Above all Lord Hugh's noble sacrifice is worth telling as an exemplar of stoicism, tenacity and bravery – a steadfast British officer born in the late Victorian era. The action at Zandvoorde was to become a watchword for selflessness and resolve in the face of overwhelming odds.

Researching the defence of Zandvoorde is challenging due to a lack of reliable sources of information. More than one hundred British soldiers were killed defending Zandvoorde. Some British soldiers on the periphery of the battle witnessed part of the action. A few of the soldiers in the doomed trenches were rendered unconscious, captured and their later accounts are less than sketchy. There were some who were wounded, or whose ammunition was spent, and were ordered to the rear before the final assault came. However there were witnesses to what happened at the end – the Germans – but they are all now dead and, by a quirk of fate, their units' war records were destroyed in the Second World War.

If there were few eye witnesses to the action at Zandvoorde is there any other evidence to shed light on what happened? There are two types of physical evidence – the trenches and the mortal remains of the fallen.

The Zandvoorde trenches were miserable muddy pits in an area which was heavily shelled for years during the war. The area has been restored to a working village in a farming area. It is therefore difficult to locate exactly where the trench line was.

What about the fallen? Only one body was known to be recovered from the trenches. The whereabouts of the others are unknown, or officially 'missing presumed dead' or more prosaically, 'known unto God'.

This book is a compilation of accounts from numerous published sources and hitherto unpublished letters from Lord Hugh and others. Inevitably there is considerable overlap in the stories told by the witnesses. The exact detail of precisely what happened at Zandvoorde will never be known. This book attempts to tell the story of those who died on that muddy ridge.

Acknowledgements

I am indebted to the Grosvenor Family for allowing me access to their archives and to numerous staff members of the Grosvenor Estate who have given their encouragement and support, especially Louise Turner and Alex Hodge.

I am most grateful for the support of John Lloyd and the Household Cavalry Museum for allowing me to reproduce images from the Christina Broom collection and to Major Brian Rogers of the Life Guards.

This book would not have been possible without the assistance of David Parkland (maps), Wayne Evans and Taff Gillingham (photographs), Charles Duthie (research material), Steve Binks (military historian) and Paul Bessemer (Lord Worsley's biographer).

I was greatly encouraged by the support from Dan Snow who graciously provided a foreword.

Foreword by Dan Snow

The terrible fighting in the autumn of 1914 is often overlooked. Lots of us seem to jump from the Retreat to the Marne and the Miracle of September to the bloody summer of 1916. The shock of the Battle of the Aisne when the British and French were cut to pieces, pinned down by immoveable Germans dug in on high ground, has been forgotten. It was there that men realised that this war would be one of trenches and sieges. We have also forgotten the vicious battles fought as autumn turned to winter on the low lying, wet coast of Belgium. Britain had entered the war to protect Belgium and now young British soldiers were hurled into makeshift defensive positions to stop the German juggernaut from conquering the whole of the country.

It was during this larger struggle that Captain Lord Hugh Grosvenor was killed, together with practically all his men. The story is so like any one of countless others from the First World War. Yet each one is unique, each one worthy of remembrance. His squadron of Life Guards was hastily deployed into poorly situated, badly-constructed, shallow trenches without the artillery support they needed to have a hope of stopping the German advance. None of them were ever found.

He was my wife's great grandfather, my children's great great grandfather. Through my children, I now have a personal connection to that intense flash of violence, a century ago, in a foreign field.

I'm so grateful to Mike McBride for writing this book. He carefully examines the circumstances of the disappearance of Grosvenor's Squadron and paints a vivid picture of the fighting to cling on to Ypres. But he also gives us a useful description of the British army in the build-up and early weeks of the war. Above all he describes a cadre of cheerful, professional, devoted men who paid an appalling price 100 years ago, and did so with a pride and conviction that is hard for many of us to imagine.

Without books like this one too many of those who died will fade like ghosts into the distant past. They deserve better. Lord Hugh is lucky that Mike has chosen to tell his story. We all are.

Dan Snow

Chapter 1

Lord Hugh William Grosvenor

Lord Hugh William Grosvenor was born on 6 April 1884 and was the eighth son of Hugh Lupus Grosvenor, 1st Duke of Westminster and his second wife Katherine Caroline Cavendish.

Hugh Lupus was educated at Eton College and Balliol College Oxford. His first wife Constance was the daughter of the Duke of Sutherland and would bear him eleven children.

Hugh Lupus Grosvenor, 1st Duke of Westminster 1825 to 1899. (*Private collection*)

In 1860 he formed the Queen's Westminster Rifle Volunteers of which he was Lieutenant Colonel and he became the Colonel Commandant of the Cheshire Yeomanry in 1869.

In 1874 the Prime Minister, William Gladstone, recommended him for a dukedom and he became the 1st Duke of Westminster. A year later his wife, Constance, contracted Bright's disease from which she died in 1880. In 1882 he married Katherine, the second daughter of Lord Chesham.

The first Duke's main concerns were improving public health, animal welfare, public access to land and sobriety. His passion was horse racing. He died in 1899 at the age of 76 and was described by George Wyndham (husband of the Duke's daughter-in-law) as 'the kindest man I ever knew'.

Lord Hugh was born into a distinguished family whose predecessors had served with distinction in the British Army. For example Thomas Grosvenor (1764–1851), the nephew of the 1st Earl Grosvenor, began his soldiering career in 1779 as Ensign in the 3rd Guards. Eventually Thomas was promoted to the highest rank the army, Field Marshal, in 1847.

Portrait of Colonel Thomas Grosvenor (later Field Marshal) in the uniform of a Lieutenant Colonel of the Grenadier Guards. (*Private collection*)

Hugh Lupus lived c1047–c1101 and is shown with a falcon on a raised gauntleted wrist as he is known for casting off and recalling his falcons as he rode on his campaigns across the Welsh border. He is seated on a horse, the model for which was bred from a Percheron mare and an English thoroughbred stallion. The statue was sculpted by George Frederick Watts. (*M. J. McBride*)

In fact all generations of the Grosvenor family had served in the military since time immemorial. Now, as in Lord Hugh's time, a magnificent statue of a nobleman on horseback graces the front of the family home, Eaton Hall in Cheshire. This statue is of Hugh Lupus who was William the Conqueror's 1st Norman Earl of Chester. The seven and a half ton bronze was commissioned by Lord Hugh's father who took an intense personal interest in ensuring that every detail of the sculpture was as historically accurate as possible. It is dated 1883, the year before Lord Hugh was born.

Lord Hugh could consider himself doubly blessed. Not only was he born into the aristocracy, but he was born British at a time when: 'The fortunes of the British Empire were at their zenith, patriotism was its watchword and nobody was questioning anything.'

Lord Hugh spent his early years at the ancestral home Eaton Hall with his elder sister Mary 'Molly' and his younger siblings Helen Frances and Edward Arthur 'Ned'.

Eaton Hall was palatial and housed a great collection of fine art. One series of tapestries by William Morris depicts incidents from Arthurian legend including Sir Lancelot fallen in battle with sword in hand. An angelic figure is featured beckoning the knight towards a door where chinks of light are shining through.

Eaton Hall circa 1880 designed by Alfred Waterhouse in 1874. (*Private Collection*)

Knights in armour
lined the staircase
inside Eaton Hall.
(*Private Collection*)

THE GRAND STAIRCASE EATON HALL   K 644

Lord Hugh was immersed in powerful chivalrous imagery – at Eaton Hall even the staircases were flanked by suits of armour. Becoming a fighting knight was his destiny. One of the highlights of the year for young Lord Hugh was the annual visit to their Scottish estate in Sutherland.

'Their governess was away on her own holiday, so they were much more with their parents than was possible at Eaton or Grosvenor House. First

The William Morris tapestry of Sir Lancelot. (*M. J. McBride*)

came the excitement of the journey from Chester in a special coach attached to the train, in which the night was spent.'

As well as deer stalking and salmon fishing from Lochmore Lodge the children enjoyed picnics on trips to Handa Island.

Deer stalking was even more challenging in Lord Hugh's time than it is now. For one thing the deer shared the mountains with grazing sheep; startled sheep would give the vigilant deer advanced warning of the approach of anyone other than an expert countryman. Lord Hugh would also not have benefited from advances in hunting rifles, ammunition and telescopic sights which modern hunters use nor today's weatherproof fabrics.

In 1899 when Lord Hugh was 15 his father, the 1st Duke of Westminster, died passing the title on to his grandson from his first marriage, Hugh Richard Arthur Grosvenor known as Bendor. Although Bendor was five years older than Lord Hugh he was, in fact, his half nephew. The Dowager Duchess of Westminster moved with her children Molly, Hugh, Frances and Ned to Combermere Abbey in Shropshire.

Molly (Mary Cavendish Grosvenor 1883–1959), Benny ('Bendor' Hugh Richard Arthur Grosvenor 1879–1953) and Hugh (Hugh William Grosvenor 1884–1914) at Lochmore Lodge, Sutherland, Scotland. (*Private collection*)

Combermere Abbey where Lord Hugh spent many of his formative years. (*Private collection*)

Lord Hugh would return to Scotland regularly for the hunting season. For example game books show that in 1910 out of the 132 stags which were culled, Lord Hugh shot a total of nine.

Lord Hugh went to Eton College near Windsor. In one of the many glowing letters to Lord Hugh's father a teacher wrote:

'Hugh is a most business like and methodical boy. He always seems to have plenty to do and never wastes time. He is very popular with the other boys, who seem to like his quiet ways and he is one of the most cheerful and good humoured of boys, with plenty to talk about but no excess of volubility, like some boys of his age. He is a very promising football player with a good deal of inexhaustible energy. I do not think I have a nicer boy in the house – he seems to be entirely ingenuous, and a most simple-minded, modest fellow. Very grateful for anything done for him and though quiet in his ways lives with plenty of purpose and go.'

Public schools of that era cultivated an ethos of team spirit, loyalty and gentlemanly honour. Schoolboys were expected not to let the side down which was epitomized in the poem *Vitai Lampada* by Sir Henry Newbolt's exhortation to 'Play up! Play up! And play the game!' This would have been well known to Lord Hugh and his contemporaries. To understand the influences on the young mind of Lord Hugh his Eton education must be considered. By his school reports it is obvious that he was an attentive student and, due to his career choice, it is likely that he had a keen interest in military history. In the annals of military history last stands like Thermopylae and do-or-die charges, such as the Charge of the Light Brigade, have a powerful grip on the public imagination. They are heart-breakingly tragic for those directly involved and, at the same time, are portrayed as heroic. They are drawn on as an inspiration for others. As an example The Alamo is ingrained into the American national psyche. The spirit of those Texan loyalists in the Alamo mission compound in San Antonio giving their lives in 1836 has inspired generations of Americans. From Greek history Lord Hugh would have learned of The Battle of Thermopylae in 480 AD where the Greek army, including 300 Spartans, defended a pass to the last man against a vastly superior Persian force. Little would he know that his own life would end in a similar 'last stand'.

History lessons involving battles between English and French knights would have undoubtedly excited the interest of Lord Hugh. Léon Gautier in his *La Chevalerie* published in 1883 tried to give a 'popular summary' of what he proposed was the 'ancient code of chivalry' of the 11th and 12th centuries. One of Gautier's Ten Commandments of chivalry included, 'Thou shalt not recoil before thine enemy.' The idea of retreating in battle was inconsistent with that of the chivalrous knight.

The term chivalry derives from the Old French term chevalerie, which can be translated to 'horse soldiery'. The horse mounted soldier has always been linked with nobility. It was not surprising therefore that the horse played a large part in the life of Lord Hugh. If the young Hugh studied the 100 Years' War he would have read of English knights under Richard II fighting in the mud of Flanders outside the town of Ypres. No-one could have predicted that he would die in battle in the same place.

One popular contemporary poem by Charles Wolfe commemorated the burial of Lieutenant General Sir John Moore at Corunna in 1809 during the Peninsular War. Moore had led a heroic withdrawal for weeks through the Galician hills fending off attacks from Napoleon's forces under Marshal Soult. This eventually led to the Battle of Elvina on 16 January 1809 where Moore was mortally wounded by French artillery. He was buried in haste by the ramparts in Corunna as his troops were evacuated, Dunkirk-style, by the Royal Navy.

The sarcophagus where Sir John Moore was re-interned is still remembered with respect by the local inhabitants of Corunna. The inscription reads, 'In memory of General Sir John Moore who fell at the Battle of Elvina while covering the embarkation of the British troops. 16th January 1809.' (*M. J. McBride*)

'No useless coffin enclosed his breast,
 Nor in sheet nor in shroud we bound him;
But he lay like a warrior taking his rest,
 With his martial cloak around him.'

The stirring poem ends:

'Slowly and sadly we laid him down,
 From the field of his fame fresh and gory;
We carv'd not a line, we raised not a stone,
 But we left him alone with his glory.'

One can speculate if the young lord was inspired by courageous leaders like Sir John Moore who selflessly sacrificed their lives even to the extent of being buried where they fell.

From the pages of British military history there are also many other examples of famous last stands where the 'thin red line' of British soldiers defended their positions against enormous odds. One such action was at the Battle of Albuera in 1811 later in the Peninsular War. Whether or not Lord Hugh learnt about Albuera at Eton, or studied the battle during his military training, is not known – but it is quite possible.

On 16 May 1811 a joint force of British, Portuguese, Spanish and German soldiers engaged the French army at the small Spanish town of Albuera, near Badajoz. In the bloodiest battle of the war there were scenes of utter carnage as the British and allied soldiers fought to stem the onslaught from Marshal Soult's French infantry and Polish lancers. At the climax of the battle Colonel Inglis, of the 1/57th West Middlesex Regiment, refused to leave his battalion although mortally wounded. Inglis encouraged his soldiers by shouting: 'Die hard, 57th, die hard!' His regiment was to become immortalized as 'The Die Hards' ever after.

Many heroic actions took place on both sides during the Battle of Waterloo on 18 June 1815. One of Napoleon's last actions was to commit the unbeaten Imperial Guard. The brave French Grand Chasseurs tried to break Wellington's line but the British 52nd Regiment, led by Lieutenant Colonel Sir John Colborne, fired volley after volley into the flank of the

Imperial Guard until they finally broke ranks and fled. The reputation of the disciplined British soldier was further enhanced by such actions.

In 1876 Colonel George Custer wrote himself into the pantheon of American heroic figures when he died with his men at Little Big Horn in his eponymous last stand. By coincidence it happened to be on the 100th anniversary of the signing of the American Declaration of Independence. Interestingly Lord Hugh was born at the same time that the Sudanese city of Khartoum was being besieged by the Mahdist forces led by Muhammed Ahmad. Khartoum was stoically defended by General Charles George Gordon but in January 1885 the city fell and Gordon was killed. Reports suggest that Gordon was in full uniform and went down fighting with pistol and sword in hand. In the aftermath of the battle Gordon came to be seen as a martyr and hero of the British Empire.

There are several last stands of which Lord Hugh would have known. On 22 January 1879, 150 British and Colonial soldiers successfully held out at Rorke's Drift in Natal against thousands of Zulu warriors led by Prince Dabulamanzi kaMpande. This steadfast action led to 11 Victoria Crosses being awarded including Lieutenants John Chard, Royal Engineers, and Gonville Bromhead, 24th Regiment of Foot.

When Lord Hugh was only nine years old an action occurred near the Shangani River in Southern Rhodesia (now Zimbabwe) which achieved prominence in Britain. In December 1893 a 34-strong mounted patrol under Major Allan Wilson encountered a force in excess of 3,000 Matabele warriors. The patrol fought to the last and was massacred. Their remains were buried next to the founder of Rhodesia, Cecil Rhodes, at World's View in the Matopos Hills near Bulawayo. In Britain a play about the Shangani Patrol 'Cheer, Boys Cheer!' toured the country for months and symbolized the performance of duty in the face of insuperable odds.

Lord Hugh was nurtured at a time when the Empire was at its peak and he was steeped in a culture which extolled fortitude and heroism. He was also one of many Grosvenors who served with distinction in the First World War. Both Lord Hugh and his older half-brother, Lord Gerald Richard Grosvenor, were destined to fight on the same battlefield: one was wounded and captured; the other paid the ultimate sacrifice.

Lord Gerald, the seventh son of the 1st Duke of Westminster, was born on 14 July 1874 at Taplow in Buckinghamshire. Like Lord Hugh he was educated at Eton College and later joined the militia (the 3rd Battalion of the Cheshire Regiment) as a subaltern (Second Lieutenant) at the age of 18 on 11 April 1893. Lord Gerald was promoted to First Lieutenant on 30 January 1895 and to Captain on 9 November 1898. On 5 July 1899 he was commissioned into the regular army in the 2nd Battalion Scots Guards as a subaltern. He served in the Anglo–Boer War 1900–1902 and fought in operations in the Orange River Colony (May to November 1900), the action at Biddulphsberg and in the Wittebergen campaign in July 1900 where he was wounded in the thigh.

On 31 December 1900 he was promoted to First Lieutenant. He was Mentioned in Despatches and received the Queen's medal with three clasps

2nd Battalion Scots Guards 24 July 1902 at Chelsea Barracks.
Back Row (left to right): W. Holbech, Master of Kinnaird, C. P. Hamilton, R. D. Fanshawe, W. Mackensie, F. C. Ricardo, M. Romer, Captain Montgomerie, N. Lechmere, Major Hanbury, Lord G. Grosvenor, Viscount Bury, H. L. Kemble, Quarter-Master Adderley, Major Ruggles-Brise.
Front Row: Capt MacLean, Surgeon-Major Beevor, Hon F. C. Gordon Lennox, Major L. G. Drummond, Major-General I. A. Trotter, Colonel Hon D. D. Hamilton, Colonel H. Flayder, Captain Master of Ruthven, Hon W. Trefusis, Captain Sergison, N. N. Nicol. (*Scots Guards*)

– Wittebergen, Cape Colony and Transvaal. On 4 January 1905 he resigned his commission.

On 10 August, only six days after war was declared, Lord Gerald rejoined the Scots Guards. In September the 2nd Battalion marched out of their barracks in the Tower of London to assemble at Lyndhurst Camp in the New Forest where they joined the 1st Battalion Grenadier Guards, 2nd Battalion Border Regiment and 2nd Battalion Gordon Highlanders to form the 20th Brigade under Brigadier General Ruggles-Brise. This was part of the 7th Division which, on 4 October, embarked at Southampton for active service in France and Belgium. In Lord Hugh's letters he refers to trying to get in touch with 'brother Gerry', but did not appear to meet up with him although they fought surprisingly closely in Flanders.

Lord Hugh had many other relatives who served in the First World War, including his younger brother Lord Edward 'Ned' Arthur Grosvenor, born 1892. Ned was educated at Eton and served as a Lieutenant in the Cheshire Yeomanry 1910–12. In May 1912 he was a subaltern in the Royal Horse Guards and, after a year, applied for a transfer to the Royal Flying Corps. In his transfer request he stated, however, that he was 'unable to serve with his own regiment owing to the fact that he gets hay fever if he goes near a horse'. This would be a debilitating condition for a cavalry officer. Ned flew with the Royal Naval Air Service and later as a Flight Commander with the Royal Flying Corps. He survived the war and became a Squadron Leader in the Auxiliary Air Force. He was awarded the Military Cross as well as being decorated by the Italian military. He died in 1929.

Lieutenant Colonel Arthur Hugh Grosvenor (1860–1929) was a son of the 1st Duke of Westminster and half-brother of Lord Hugh. He commanded the Cheshire Yeomanry in the Boer War. In 1914 he was appointed to command the home-based 3rd Battalion of the Cheshire Regiment. His wife, Lady Arthur Grosvenor, supervised the Red Cross military hospital which was set up at Eaton Hall during the First World War.

Captain Robert Arthur Grosvenor (1895–1953) was the son of Lieutenant Colonel Arthur Hugh Grosvenor and joined the Cheshire Yeomanry with duties in the Welsh Mounted Border Brigade. In 1915 he transferred into a regular cavalry regiment, the Queen's Bays, and later the Royal Flying

Lord Edward 'Ned' Grosvenor leaving Combermere Abbey. Note the hunting rifle attached to the side of his cockpit and the caption, 'Landing and nearly killing the photographer who knew even less than I did about aeroplanes'. (*Private Collection*)

LEAVING ENGLAND FOR THE FRONT
AUGUST 1914.

LANDING, AND NEARLY KILLING THE
PHOTOGRAPHER WHO KNEW EVEN
LESS THAN I DID ABOUT AEROPLANES.

Corps. By 1918 he had won the Military Cross (and bar) and had been Mentioned in Despatches.

Lord Hugh's half-nephew was the 2nd Duke of Westminster, Hugh Richard Arthur Grosvenor; he was better known as Bendor and served in the Royal Horse Guards in the Anglo-Boer War where he was Mentioned in Despatches.

Hugh Richard Arthur Grosvenor the 2nd Duke of Westminster – 'Bendor'. In the uniform of the Royal Horse Guards following service in the Anglo-Boer War. (*Private Collection*)

Bendor had a full and colourful life. His passion for competitive horse racing ended in 1904 when he fell whilst riding in the Grand National. At the outbreak of the First World War he rejoined his regiment and, without hesitation or waiting for official orders, went to France. He rescued Captain Francis Grenfell of the 9th Lancers whilst under fire. When writing about the death of his half-brother Percy Wyndham he wrote, 'He went in good company with several of his friends in a way most befitting him, with a heap of Germans slain around him.'

Bendor was a liaison officer on Sir John French's staff until November 1914 when he took command of a squadron of six Rolls-Royce armoured cars which he had purchased himself. After distinguished service on the Western Front he crossed to North Africa with his armoured cars. There in 1916 he won the Distinguished Service Order for rescuing the crew of the torpedoed ship *Tara* who were being held captive by Senussi tribesmen in the Egyptian desert.

Serving King and Empire was not the sole prerogative of the male Grosvenors. The first wife of Bendor, Constance Cornwallis-West (1877– 1970) founded and ran the Constance, Duchess of Westminster, Hospital in Le Touquet France throughout the war for which she was decorated.

Lord Hugh would serve with many fellow officers who were linked by birth, marriage or social connection. A good example of this was Lieutenant Colonel His Highness the Duke of Teck, later to adopt the appellation Adolphus Cambridge, 1st Marquess of Cambridge in 1917 when anti-German sentiment caused many with German names to Anglicize them. The Duke of Teck was the younger brother of Queen Mary and was married to Lord Hugh's half-sister Margaret.

It is hardly surprising that Lord Hugh joined the cavalry. It would have been more surprising if he had not. The most senior units in the British Army are its cavalry regiments: The most senior cavalry regiment was the First Regiment of Life Guards (1/Life Guards or 1/LG). By 1912 1/LG was the most exclusive regiment in the army, nearly three quarters of its officers had titles and one in five were from the landed gentry. The Household Cavalry drew heavily on old Etonians and the nominal roll contained the crème de la crème of aristocratic families such as the Astors, Carletons, Castlereaghs,

Lieutenant Colonel His
Highness the Duke of Teck.
(*Christina Broom*)

Lt. Col.H.H.The Duke of Teck.
1st Life Guards.

Cavendishes, Hoares, Leveson–Gowers, Montgomeries, Pagets, Pelhams, Thymes, Wyndhams as well as Grosvenors. It was the obvious choice for Lord Hugh, the son of the Duke of Westminster, who was a cadet at the Royal Military College Sandhurst and commissioned into 1/LG as Second Lieutenant on 27 May 1903. At Sandhurst successful candidates for commissions in the army have to express their preference for the regiment in which they would like to serve. Lord Hugh opted for 1/LG as his first preference and the RHG as his second. Under his signature his senior officer endorsed his application with typical understatement: 'Will make a good soldier.'

Upon joining his regiment Lord Hugh would have been fully employed as a troop leader in training exercises as well as ceremonial duties. Cavalry training at Windsor was described by a trooper:

'The whole regiment left barracks daily in the early morning and returned covered with dust and sweat about 1 pm. I found these excursions thrilling. There was much galloping. To gallop in the ranks in various formations, but especially in line with the whole regiment, was sheer joy. Horses soon became hard and fit. To see them at work and to work with them made life worth living.'

This training led on to more tactical exercises or 'schemes':

'The Regiment went out after imaginary enemy, sometimes represented by half-a-dozen mounted men carrying flags. In these games we

First Lieutenants Wyndham, Fellowes and Grosvenor at Pirbright in August 1905. The cavalry spent a month each year at Pirbright on musketry training. (*Private collection*)

were taught the duties of scouts, and advance, flank and rear-guards. Dismounted action played a large part. Riflemen, panting and perspiring, doubled for miles over the countryside while, some distance behind, the number-threes struggled with armfuls of contrary led horses each one of which seemed to have its own ideas as to the best way of conducting the battle. It was all very strenuous, but excellent training.

'When a section of horses and their riders went into action dismounted they allocated the third rider (the number-three) the hapless job of restraining the riderless mounts.'

Within a year Lord Hugh was promoted to First Lieutenant on 4 February 1904. He evidently was a born horseman and thrived on sporting activities. As well as working with horses in the Life Guards he also had a passion for racing, hunting and was an excellent polo player.

Lord Hugh was an accomplished jockey and rode in point-to-point races. (*Private collection*)

As an active equestrian sporting injuries were an occupational hazard for Lord Hugh. (*Private collection*)

Whilst on leave from regimental duties, Lord Hugh often went hunting. He would have had an active London 'Season' of social events as well as engagements in the country. For example at Oulton Park Hall,

> 'The highlights of winters were "bachelors ordinaries", when each Saturday a bachelor in Cheshire would give a dinner party for the rest of his circle of friends at his home. No ladies were allowed and only the occasional married man as a special compliment. A strong constitution was required, as the dinner was preceded by a hard day's hunting followed by gambling and a long, cold, ride home.'

Lord Hugh and his contemporaries were hardened and fit by a strenuous sporting life.

1903 draghound season. Captain H.M. Walker Master of Hounds in the centre of the photograph with Lord Hugh Grosvenor 1st Whip on the right. (*Household Cavalry Museum*)

In April 1906 Lord Hugh married Mabel Horatia Mary Crichton at St Peter's Church, Eaton Square, London. Mabel was the second daughter of the 4th Earl of Erne. This church in Belgravia was a popular choice for society weddings. A few years earlier Lord Hugh's half-brother Lord Arthur Grosvenor was best man at the wedding of Sir Philip Brian Grey-Egerton of Oulton Hall to Mae Cuyler. Oulton Hall was the birthplace of twin brothers Philip de Malpas Wayne Egerton and Rowland le Belward Egerton who were both killed in action in the First World War.

Second Lieutenant Rowland le Belward Egerton (1/RWF) and twin brother Second Lieutenant Philip de Malpas Wayne Egerton. (*Cheshire Yeomanry*)

St Peter's Church, Eaton Square, London. (*M. J. McBride*)

Lord and Lady Hugh Grosvenor lived at 9 Southwick Crescent (now called Hyde Park Crescent) across the park from the barracks at Knightsbridge. They had two children, Gerald Hugh Grosvenor (later 4th Duke of Westminster) and Robert George Grosvenor (later 5th Duke of Westminster).

On 31 January 1911 Lord Hugh was guest at the wedding of Lieutenant Charles Sackville Pelham, Lord Worsley, at Westminster Abbey to the Honourable Alexandra Mary Freesia Vivian, who was the sister of Sir Douglas Haig's wife, Dorothy. Another distinguished guest, old Etonian and fellow Life Guard, was Captain Alexander Moore Vandeleur.

Destiny would bring Lord Hugh, Lord Worsley and Captain Vandeleur together in a fatal encounter in Flanders in 1914.

An informal gathering of family and friends c.1911. (*Private collection*)

Back Row: Colonel W. Lambton, Duke of Roxburghe, Cyril Ward, Lord Dudley, F. Grenfell, Lord Hugh Grosvenor.

Middle Row: Lord Willoughby de Eresby, Lady Willoughby de Eresby, Lady Crichton, Lady Ridly, Duchess Roxburghe, G. Ward.

Front Row: A. Stanley, Lady Evelyn Ward, Lady Mabel Grosvenor, Lord Crichton.

Lord Hugh seated
with wife Lady
Mabel Grosvenor,
their son Gerald
and friends. (*Private
collection*)

Noblesse oblige – As a member of the aristocracy Lord Hugh would be asked to present prizes
at local sporting events such as here at a soccer match in 1911. (*Private collection*)

1903 Life Guards Polo Team.
Back Row (mounted): left to right Guest, Carden, Fraser, Cavendish, Henderson, Newry.
Standing: Darrel, Waring, Grosvenor, Eyre, Calley, Milner, Clowes, Cookson, Brassey, Stubber, Fellowes.
Seated: Meredith, Stanley, Walker. (*Household Cavalry Museum*)

Officers of 1/Life Guards in 1906 at Combermere Barracks, Windsor.
Standing left to right: Lupton, Stubber, Grosvenor, Parker, Guest, Newry, Fellowes, Monckton, Gifford, Mundy, Wyndham, Meredith, Hardy, Astor, Hall, Yeatman
Seated: Carden, Walker, Shute, Bingham, Oliphant, Calley, Milner, Brassey, Stanley, Deeble, Cavendish
Front: Cook, Cookson (*Household Cavalry Museum*)

1906 Polo match between the Life Guards and the Royal Horse Guards (RHG) or the 'Blues'.
Back row left to right: Carden, Foster, Bowlby (RHG), Herbert, Grosvenor, Wyndham.
Third row: Stanley.
Second row: Stubber, Mundy, Rose (RHG), J.Fitzgerald (RHG), Gerard (RHG), Angelsey (RHG), Mann-Thompson (RHG), H.Brassey (RHG), Newry, Harrison (RHG), Monkton, Gifford, Eyre.
Front row: Naper, Innes-Ker (RHG), Guest, Wilson (RHG), Milner, Fenwick (RHG), Calley, G.Fitzgerald (RHG), Cookson, E.Brassey, Cavendish. (*Household Cavalry Museum*)

1907 Polo match between the Life Guards and the Royal Horse Guards.
Back row left to right: Gerard, Astor, Stubber, Fellowes, Grosvenor, Howard-Vyse (RHG), Somers, E.Brassey, Wyndham, Mundy, Harrison (RHG)
Middle row: Hardy, Stanley, Dromore, Bowlby (RHG), Drage (RHG), H.Brassey (RHG), Newry, Rose (RHG), Eyre, Monckton, Innes-Ker (RHG)
Front row: Carden, Herbert (RHG), Fitzgerald (RHG), A of Teck, Fenwick (RHG), Milner, Mann-Thompson (RHG), Cookson, Crichton (RHG), Naper (RHG). (*Household Cavalry Museum*)

Life Guards polo team. Lord Hugh third from left. (*Private collection*)

The historic purpose of the Life Guards was to protect the Sovereign. Lord Hugh did his share of 'public duties' and took part in the annual Trooping the Colour ceremony at Horse Guards Parade, London.

On 22 June 1911 Lord Hugh served as part of the escort for the Coronation of His Majesty King George V and Queen Mary at Westminster Abbey.

Demonstrating the close pre-war bonds between the British and German aristocracy the seventh carriage in the royal procession that day contained Duke Albrecht of Württemberg and Prince Rupprecht of Bavaria. At Ypres little more than three years later the German Fourth Army was commanded by the former and the German Sixth Army was led by the latter.

1907 Trooping the Colour past the Sovereign King Edward VII on Horse Guards Parade, London. Captain H. M. Walker, Captain P. B. Cookson, Lieutenant Lord Newry, Lieutenant G. Mundy, Lieutenant Lord Hugh Grosvenor, Second Lieutenant Lord Somers. (*Household Cavalry Museum*)

The standard for turnout in the Life Guards was then, and is now, immaculate. (*Christina Broom*)

When not looking after their horses or applying spit-and-polish to their own kit the Life Guardsmen could have a rare moment of relaxation in barracks. (*Christina Broom*)

The three regiments which made up the Household Cavalry, namely the 1st and 2nd Regiments of Life Guards and the Royal Horse Guards (RHG) were based at the Knightsbridge Barracks and Regents Park Barracks in London and Combermere Barracks in Windsor. The regiments rotated between the barracks annually.

Whilst based at Knightsbridge Barracks one trooper in 1/LG took out a couple of spare horses for exercise in the early mornings with Sergeant 'Cabby' Dawes and gives a flavour of what peacetime soldiering was like. Initially the morning canters were confined to Hyde Park then Cabby had the idea of going through the London backstreets where they supped milk and rum at a local pub:

Knightsbridge Barracks, Hyde Park, London. (*Christina Broom*)

'It was the beginning of the end of our outings for very soon they showed signs of developing into a common pub-crawl. I decided Cabby would be better off in bed, so in bed I left him. He was a charming fellow … he was lost with many another good fellow on Zandvoorde ridge.'

Officers' inspection of the C Squadron 1/LG stables at Knightsbridge Barracks. (*Christina Broom*)

LIFE GUARDS FIRST DUTY

A special bond existed between the cavalryman and his 'Pal'. (*Christina Broom*)

The final pay parade at Knightsbridge Barracks administered by Corporal Major Gulliver and Major John Cavendish DSO (seated without hat). (*Christina Broom*)

On 13 May 1908 Lord Hugh was promoted to Captain.

Captain Lord Hugh William Grosvenor, 1/Life Guards in cavalry service dress at Knightsbridge Barracks in August 1914. At this stage the badges of rank, three metal bath stars or 'pips', were prominently worn on each epaulette on the shoulder. Later in the war officers wore their rank more discreetly on their cuffs. (*Christina Broom*)

Chapter 2

The British Army of 1914

Britain at the turn of the century in 1900 was on the brink of massive change. The change affected the Empire as it adapted to revolutionary restructuring and came to terms with the modern world. The next two decades would see royal dynasties crumble, borders be re-drawn and new nations emerge. Centuries of social norms would be cast aside, women became emancipated and class became less important. At home in the 1900s Britain saw the end of the certainties of the Victorian era.

In military terms the Royal Navy had the largest fleet of warships in the world and was building new battleships called Dreadnoughts to counter the perceived threat from the German Navy.

The British Army last saw action on mainland Europe nearly 100 years previously in 1815 at the Battle of Waterloo. It was licking its wounds following the costly Anglo-Boer War in South Africa and was embarking on widespread reforms in equipment and tactics.

Its regimental system fostered an ethos of loyalty and team spirit. Joining a regiment was akin to joining a family: 'A family who would risk their lives for each other. What made the British Army formidable were the fighting qualities of its soldiers.' The close-knit bond of the regimental system was a double-edged sword as described by Sir Anthony Farrar-Hockley:

'The regiment was the strength of the British Army but in a sense its weakness. Unique amongst the armies of the Powers of Europe, the British was a wholly professional body; all its officers and men were long-service volunteers as distinct from conscripts. The result was a high standard of training in weapons, field-craft and map-reading and an exemplary discipline; the standards being enhanced by service in a series of minor colonial wars. Close bonds of friendship bound officers and soldiers due to their long association together in and out of the firing line. A company commander in an infantry battalion would find as his company sergeant-major a man with whom he had soldiered intermittently for 20 years. He would know every man in the battalion as a whole by name and many by number. On joining, it was made clear to the cavalry or infantry subaltern that the regiment was the prime interest in his life … In consequence the quality of officers entering the staff colleges at Camberley or Quetta was not high and the quality of the syllabus and methods were equally mediocre.'

Whereas the British leadership of battalions or regiments was exemplary, the strategic handling of Divisions, Corps and Armies could be questionable. Due to the global deployment of the Army throughout the British Empire, and the dubious quality of staff officer training, senior officers did not work sufficiently well with their counterparts. They were not inoculated against military genius, but the experience of the First World War did identify serious shortcomings in their strategic ability.

In 1904 a member of the Elgin Commission, setup to learn lessons from the Anglo-Boer War, claimed unkindly that 'only two out of forty regimental officers were any good at all. The rest were loafers.' Whether the accusation was in fact true is impossible to determine. What is true was the incredible pace of change in the British Army, especially its officer corps, from 1902 to 1914. Lord Hugh would have witnessed unprecedented improvements in the professionalism of the army as it came to terms with technological advances in military science and doctrine.

The spirit of the fighting man in 1914 was different to the ones who would follow. This is summed up by historian Lyn Macdonald as 'resignation to dying, their passive embracement of fate, their unquestioning acceptance. The questioning and bitterness were born later, in the stultifying horrors of trench warfare.'

John Buchan encapsulated the British Army of 1914:

'Perhaps the most wonderful fighting man that the world has seen. Officers and men were curiously alike. Behind all the differences of birth and education there was a common temperament; a kind of humourous realism about life, a dislike of talk, a belief in inherited tradition and historical ritual, a rough-and-ready justice, a deep cheerfulness which was not inconsistent with a surface pessimism. They generally took a dark view of the immediate prospect; therefore they were never seriously depressed. They had an unshakable confidence in the ultimate issue; therefore they never thought it worth mentioning. They were always slightly puzzled; therefore they could never be completely at a loss; for the man who insists on having the next steps neatly outlined before he starts will be unnerved if he cannot see his way; whereas others will drive on cheerfully into the mist, because they have been there before, and know that on the further side there is clear sky.'

The performance of the British soldier was summed up succinctly by an officer of the German General Staff:

'The Englishman is cool and indifferent to danger … he stays where he is commanded … he shoots magnificently, extraordinarily well … it is when luck is against him that he is at his very best.'

During the Anglo-Boer War (1899–1902) the

'dismal performance of scouting duties … prompted a complete overhaul of reconnaissance organization, while innovative training methods were introduced to improve scouting and horse-manship.'

In the cavalry there were two competing schools of thought during this period, the 'cold steel and lance' brigade championed by Sir John French and Sir Douglas Haig and the 'dismounted tactics' favoured by Lord Roberts. By 1909 the Army were thinking ahead and may have predicted that the advent of military technology, such as the Maxim machine gun, would effectively sound the death knell of the traditional cavalryman. One of the lessons the British Army learnt from the Boer *Kommandos* was the value of having rapidly mobile mounted soldiers who could also fight dismounted as infantrymen. Accordingly the cavalry were issued with the Short Magazine Lee-Enfield (SMLE) rifle and expected to be as proficient in marksmanship as their infantry comrades. This is exactly what Lord Hugh was employed doing when defending Ypres. As one officer of the general staff put it:

'The training of the cavalry with the rifle has been invaluable, and has given them great advantage over the enemy.'

Morgan Crofton echoed this sentiment:

'When we remember the storm which arose ... when it was first proposed that cavalry should be armed with the rifle, we cannot help feeling thankful that this arming was carried out, although in the teeth of the fiercest opposition. The possession of this weapon has conferred

Instructor training Life Guardsmen the principles of marksmanship with the Short Magazine Lee-Enfield rifle. (*Christina Broom*)

very great power on the cavalry. It was owing to this power that we were able to screen the sorely stricken infantry, and keep the hostile masses at the proper distance.'

Wavell suggested that

'it is not too much to say that the fate of the war depended on the fact that this cavalry had been trained to use the rifle with an effect that no horseman or infantry in other European armies could match.'

The superiority of British musketry during 1914 has become legendary. In the official German account of the First Battle of Ypres the British were credited with: 'Quantities of machine guns,' 'large numbers of machine guns' with the effect that 'the roads were swept by machine guns', and that 'over every bush, hedge and fragment of wall floated a thin film of smoke betraying a machine gun rattling out bullets.' Actually in the First Battle of Ypres machine guns were quite scarce. Each infantry battalion or cavalry regiment was only equipped with two machine guns; these were often unserviceable due to a lack of spare parts. The British General Staff concluded that the 'rapid fire of the British rifleman … was mistaken for machine-gun fire both as regards volume and effect.'

The French and German cavalry still issued their troopers with short barrelled rifles known as carbines. These carbines were not as accurate or as effective at battlefield ranges as the trusty SMLE which had a detachable box magazine of ten rounds of .303 inch ammunition whereas the French and German rifles only held five rounds. 'The British were accustomed regularly to firing at 800 yards … and many could hit a man approaching at 1,000 yards.'

In 1902 the German Kaiser was so keen on the Maxim machine-gun that, at his own expense, he equipped his cavalry units with them. In 1910 Major General Edmund Allenby was appointed Inspector General of Cavalry and oversaw dramatic improvements in all aspects of war fighting both in terms of horse-mastery and marksmanship. These advances made by the irascible Allenby led to the British cavalry being considered massively superior to their German counterparts.

British Army regiments of 1914 were equipped with two Maxim or Vickers machine guns per regiment. Incidentally the German Army were equipped with an almost identical weapon. The Maxims were replaced by the Vickers machine gun, Mark 1. (*Taff Gillingham*)

Vickers machine-gun, Mark 1. (*Imperial War Museum*)

Horse-mastery improved dramatically between 1902 and 1914. For example, horses were allowed to graze when they could and the British cavalryman walked as much as he rode. The German and French cavalry had a bad habit of staying mounted unnecessarily, especially while moving along hard road surfaces leading to lameness in the horses. It has been noted that

'the reform of reconnaissance and horse-mastery in the 1902–14 period was a quiet success story for the British Cavalry.'

There is a common perception that the use of cavalry in the First World War was a 'touchstone of all that is … foolish and futile.' However the British Cavalry were invaluable, especially in the first few months. Although ceremonial duties played a large part of regimental life the cavalry also had an operational role as the vanguard of the army. Cavalry scouted ahead of the army as the 'eyes and ears' of their commander as well covering the exposed flanks of an army on the move. The 1890 manual of Modern Tactics noted that 'for reconnoitering purposes, in pursuit, and during a retreat, cavalry is absolutely essential.'

Lieutenant General Edmund Allenby. (*Imperial War Museum*)

Reconnaissance was divided into three disciplines:

Strategic Reconnaissance where both armies were distant,
Tactical Reconnaissance where the armies were in striking distance of each other,
and Protective Reconnaissance to intercept enemy patrols.

The British Cavalry in 1914 were able to conduct effective reconnaissance operations including long distance scouting as well as tenacious fighting. The cavalry could operate independent of infantry support. The final phase of scouting was normally done dismounted and the British Cavalryman was well trained and equipped to do this having adopted lessons from the Anglo–Boer War. The cavalry, however, did not have the monopoly on reconnaissance work. As the First World War progressed, other parts of the army shared this burden. Captain Sir Morgan Crofton, 6th Baronet of Mohill, was in charge of the machine-gun and signals sections of 2/LG and commented:

> 'In this war, the work of reconnaissance, which is one of cavalry's chief roles, has largely been done by aeroplanes and motorcycles.'

Before the days of aeroplanes, helicopter gunships, paratroopers and special forces the cavalry were the shock troops of their day. Their massed charges were used to strike terror into the heart of the enemy. Cavalry were the spearhead of the army – the so-called *Arme Blanche*.

By 1914 the British Army was in a state of transformation. Although at a strategic level there may have been room for improvement, at regimental level it was world class. In terms of scale, however, the British Army was puny compared with the behemoths of the French, German, Austro-Hungarian and Russian armies. Had it embraced the lessons of the Russo-Japanese War of 1904–1905, the Manchurian War, the ethos of the British Army would have favoured defence rather than attack. It would have therefore trained in entrenching and equipped itself with more artillery and machine guns.

Chapter 3

British Expeditionary Force (BEF)

Britain had an excellent army, but it was ill-prepared for the sort of war in which it found itself in 1914. According to James Edmonds the BEF was: 'Incomparably the best trained, best organised and best equipped British Army that ever went forth to war.' This all-volunteer, well trained, well equipped force of seasoned professional soldiers was an elite. At the outbreak of war Sir Douglas Haig advocated that the BEF should be used as a nucleus on which to build a mass army rather than commit it straight into the conflict. Haig appeared to have the prescient belief that the war would not be over by Christmas but would be a long hard slog. There was, however, an imperative to deploy the BEF immediately and Haig's view was ignored. The BEF was a regular formation consisting of a cavalry division, two infantry corps together with artillery and other supporting arms which would have been more than capable of projecting the nation's power around the empire to deal with the 'little wars' of which Britain had decades of experience. The army was much like a colonial police force and was used to fighting inferior opposition.

A Corps usually consisted of two Divisions; a Division comprised three Brigades; an infantry Brigade normally had four battalions; and a cavalry Brigade four regiments.

A cavalry regiment in 1914 comprised of the following:

Regimental Headquarters numbering 7 officers and 35 other ranks;
A Machine-Gun Section, with two machine guns consisting of 25 men and 4 officers;
3 Squadrons, each of 7 officers and 159 other ranks; each squadron was divided into four troops, which numbered 1 officer and 28 other ranks.

In comparison with the massive French and German armies the BEF was minute. In fact Kaiser Wilhelm II was reported as referring to the BEF as the 'contemptible little army'. In only the way the good humoured British soldier can, the veterans of the BEF adopted this derogatory epithet and cheerfully called themselves, 'The Old Contemptibles'.

As the war progressed the British Army was bolstered by the regular regiments shipped back from far flung outposts of Empire (especially India); former soldiers (reservists) were recalled to the colours; territorials signed up for Imperial Service; the Empire rallied to the motherland and thousands of soldiers from dominions such as South Africa, Rhodesia, Canada, Newfoundland, Australia, New Zealand and India answered the call; thousands of Chinese men formed labour battalions; Lord Kitchener recruited a new volunteer army which would first see action in 1915 at Loos; in 1916 conscription was brought in to coerce young men to join the military; and eventually American 'Doughboys' under General Pershing joined the war. These additions, however, apart from reservists were of no use to the BEF in 1914. It had to get into the fight with the available resources. Regular British Army units were also rushed across the Channel to augment the BEF. Lord Hugh was in one such draft of reinforcements.

Field Marshal Sir John French, later Viscount French of Ypres, commanded the BEF. (*Imperial War Museum*)

Lieutenant General (later Field Marshal) Sir Douglas Haig later Earl Haig initially commanded I Corps of the BEF and eventually became Chief of the Imperial General Staff. (*Imperial War Museum*)

The BEF (bolstered by other regular army units) was to fill a pivotal role in the opening months of the war and, although on occasions they were forced to withdraw to keep in line with their French allies, their line was never broken comprehensively. It was though a close run thing.

The Commander-in-Chief of the BEF was Field Marshal Sir John French. Major General (later Lieutenant General) Edmund Allenby commanded the Cavalry Division (later to become the Cavalry Corps). I Corps was commanded by Lieutenant General (later Field Marshal) Sir Douglas Haig and II Corps was commanded by Lieutenant General Sir Horace Smith-Dorrien who had taken command on 21 August after the death of Lieutenant General Sir James Grierson a few days earlier.

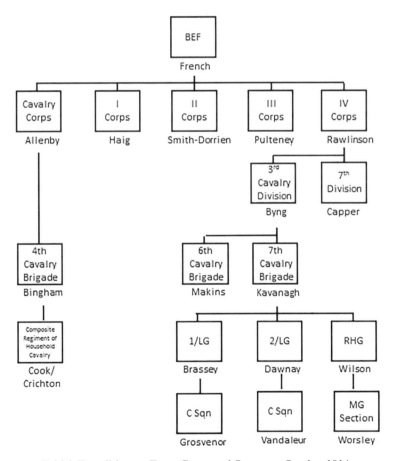

British Expeditionary Force Command Structure October 1914.

A popular perception of the First World War was that the British soldiers were lions led by Generals who were characterized as donkeys. In the last 100 years Haig has been particularly associated with the donkey epithet as being a butcher and bungler. Although Haig and his contemporaries made mistakes, the 'donkey' label is unfair and inaccurate.

III Corps under Major General William Pulteney was formed in France at the end of August and comprised of the 4th and 6th infantry divisions which had landed in France in August and September respectively.

In October 1/LG, with Lord Hugh, was part of IV Corps under Lieutenant General Sir Henry Rawlinson and consisted of the 7th Infantry Division led by Major General Thompson Capper and the 3rd Cavalry Division commanded by Major General J. H. G. Byng.

The 3rd Cavalry Division had two brigades, the 6th and 7th Cavalry Brigade, commanded by Brigadier General C. T. Kavanagh, consisted of 1/LG, 2/LG and RHG also known as the 'Blues'.

To complicate matters still further, at the outbreak of war it was decided to supplement the BEF with a regiment of cavalry. This regiment was made up of a squadron from each of the three regiments in the Household Brigade and was known as the Composite Regiment of Household Cavalry under the command of Lieutenant Colonel Edwin Cook. They would leave for France in August as part of the 4th Cavalry Brigade under Brigadier General C. E. Bingham.

Corporal of Horse Lloyd in 1/LG wrote:

'A Composite Regiment of Household Cavalry was formed at once, each regiment contributing one service squadron of four sixteen-file troops. In addition, our regiment provided the Headquarters of the Composite Regiment. The effort pretty well cleared out the whole of the old regiment. … Those that we left behind would be made up to strength with reservists and retain the title of 1st Life Guards.'

For 1/LG to donate its Headquarters Squadron and one of its three squadrons to the Composite Regiment must have been a significant loss. Peacetime strengths of regular units were often far less than they should have been and the shortfall in the establishment was made up of reservists

Lieutenant Colonel Edwin Berkeley Cook M.V.O. 1/Life Guards preparing to depart Knightsbridge Barracks, London, with his Composite Regiment of Household Cavalry. (*Christina Broom*)

recalled to the colours. In October Lord Hugh mentioned in a letter, with eager anticipation, that the Composite Regiment was being disbanded and the men returning to their parent regiments. This happened on 11 November 1914 – too late for Lord Hugh to see it. It seems obvious that the transfer of experienced 1/LG officers, non-commissioned officers and troopers to the Composite Regiment was keenly felt.

The 7th Cavalry Brigade had to be brought up to full strength, or 'wartime establishment'. Vacancies in 1/LG were filled with reservists who belonged to 'slightly less exclusive regiments known by the Army as the Cavalry of the Line.' So although Lord Hugh, on paper, commanded a squadron of Life Guardsmen it included a good many former dragoon guards and dragoons. Although these reservists may not have been exactly the same calibre as the

The 1/Life Guards on parade in their dismounted role as infantrymen. Note the absence of steel helmets, the cavalry swords which they still had to carry and the improvised way of carrying their equipment slung across themselves in a blanket roll or greatcoat. These soldiers were photographed in 1917, but would have been similar to those of 1914 apart from the bayonets which were by now standard issue. (*Christina Broom*)

Life Guards, they were seasoned soldiers who may have seen service in India or even South Africa – 'they were useful men … they were hard riders and sharpshooters. They would do.'

If there was a temptation for the elite Life Guardsmen to look down their noses at the reservists from the Dragoon Guards the feeling was mutual:

'As a whole [the Dragoon Guards] rather resented being attached to us at first. They accused their own regiments of breach of faith in casting them out. They had a high opinion of their own value as soldiers, and their main grievance was that they had been drafted to a miserable regiment of tin soldiers in order to prevent us by their gallantry and soldierly qualities from disgracing ourselves when we come into action. Anyway, their behaviour was, to put it very mildly somewhat wild. For all their wild and woolly ways, they were fine soldiers and good fellows, apart from a small gang of toughs. We came to live, and later die, with them in perfect harmony.'

Initially the Dragoon Guards referred to their Life Guard hosts as Piccadilly Cowboys or Ticky Tins. Captain George Arthur of 2/LG wrote,

'This strange assortment of regiments welded together, and people may have smiled to see men of five feet four inches wearing the badge of the Household Cavalry; but however small their stature, they were to add robustly to the reputation of their adopted regiments, and at the same time to admit that they themselves had gained by inclusion in them, and by being able to take the correct measure of comrades whom they might previously have regarded as feather-bed soldiers.'

The amount of equipment carried by each cavalryman and horse was substantial. By 1914 the marching order for the cavalry trooper was heavy. His average total weight on horseback was about eighteen stone. He wore a stiff-peaked khaki cap, a khaki serge jacket, breeches, puttees, black leather ankle-boots and spurs. Over his left shoulder he carried a bandolier with thirty rounds of .303 ammunition and a felt-covered water bottle. Over his right shoulder was slung a haversack, which seldom actually contained a regulation knife, fork and spoon. Each horse carried round its neck a leather bandolier with a further sixty rounds of ammunition. The .303 Short, Magazine, Lee-Enfield Rifle rested in its leather rifle-bucket on the offside. To the saddle were strapped a flat, round metal mess-tin and a feedbag with seven pounds of oats. Finally, other ranks also carried the Cavalry Pattern 1908 sword (officers carried the 1912 Pattern Cavalry Sword) in its metal

Lieutenant John Close-Brooks was one of Lord Hugh's troop leaders in C Squadron. (*Christina Broom*)

scabbard, with leather frog to which was also attached a horseshoe-shaped leather case containing two horseshoes and nails. Another seven-pound feedbag was on the near side with a folding canvas bucket. On the saddle's front arch was a pair of leather wallets for small kit with a rolled mackintosh

Captain Gerrard Leigh and men of 1/LG preparing for operational deployment. Lord Hugh would have been kitted out like Captain Leigh. The absence of an ammunition bandolier across his chest indicates that he would not have been armed with a SMLE .303 rifle, but would have carried a six-shot service revolver in addition to his sword. He is also carrying a map case which Lord Hugh mentions in his last letter home. There is also a wooden stake to be driven into the ground to tether his horse in the field. (*Christina Broom*)

cape over them and on the rear arch a rolled greatcoat. Under the saddle was one blanket for the man and another for the horse.

Military preparations for the British Army were meticulously prescribed in the War Book which detailed every action needed to get soldiers into their battle positions:

> 'It was all laid down, from the method of packing his dress uniform for storage to a stern reminder that the book he was reading must be returned to the garrison library.'

The War Book would have found favour with staff officers and anyone who finds comfort in complexity. However the war plans of all of the armies were in disarray by the end of 1914. It confirms the saying of German General Helmuth von Moltke that 'no plan survives first contact with the enemy.' This was illustrated vividly on 18 September when Haig visited the wounded in a makeshift field hospital and found that even basics such as dressings and stretchers were in short supply: 'The situation is quite unlike what the regulations anticipated!'

On mobilization officers were kept busy with administrative tasks; one exasperated officer noted 'I am kept busy checking kit, filling in documents and doing the hundred and one things that are necessary before a regiment can proceed on active service.'

In preparation for deployment the 7th Division assembled at Lyndhurst Camp in the New Forest 10 miles west of Southampton. Essentially the 7th Division, and the 3rd Cavalry Division, represented some of the last of the regular army to reinforce the embattled BEF across The Channel. On 27 August Major General Sir Thompson Capper was appointed as the General Officer Commanding the 7th Division. 'Tommy' Capper was not only a veteran of several military campaigns, but was a fervent exponent of the benefits of the offensive strategy in warfare. The tactics employed in the First Battle of Ypres can be understood by studying Capper's experience and views.

Thompson Copeland Capper was born in 1863 in Lucknow, India which still bore the scars of the Indian Mutiny of 1857. Tommy's father, although a civilian, fought with distinction to defend Lucknow. Bravery was clearly a family character trait. In 1882 Capper was commissioned into the 1st Battalion of the East Lancashire Regiment and he saw action in 1895 in the Chitral expedition. In 1898 he was chosen to join the Sudanese Army and fought at the Battle of Arbara and at Omdurman where he led a successful attack against the odds. Tommy was again in action throughout the Anglo-Boer War leading mobile columns and being awarded the Distinguished Service Order, six Mentions in Despatches and several other decorations. In 1902 Capper was appointed as professor at the Staff College at Camberley where he revolutionized the teaching. In particular

Major General Thompson Copeland Capper. (*Imperial War Museum*)

'he always inculcated a spirit of self-sacrifice and duty, instead of playing for safety and seeking only to avoid getting into trouble. This high-minded inspiration marked all the teaching under Rawlinson too, but it was due perhaps more to Capper than to anyone else. It was like a silver thread which ran through every problem we discussed and studied.'

In Capper's own lecture notes he extolled the virtue of self-sacrifice:

'The art of war consists almost entirely in the application of one principle; that principle never changes. It is the principle that determination to conquer or die must pervade all ranks …'

This spirit of 'conquer or die' espoused by Capper was not uncommon in the officer corps of the 1914 British Army. He also went on to advocate a 'vigorous and uncompromising offensive attitude.' Tommy Capper was no armchair strategist – he practised what he preached by an appetite for risk and always leading from the front. His instinct was to lead by example and demonstrate his personal courage. He was a paradigm of the late Victorian officer class.

Capper's formative combat experiences gained in India, the Sudan and South Africa were supplemented by a study of the Manchurian War of 1907. The tactic of both Russian and Japanese commanders of siting their trenches on the forward slopes was applauded by Capper, although it exposed the front line to enemy artillery fire. Following the spirit of the likes of Capper the trench was seen almost as a jumping off point to launch an attack on the enemy rather than as a bulwark against which enemy forces would be smashed. Contemporary accounts of pre-war training proved that the British Army were preparing for a skirmishing war on open ground similar to the Anglo-Boer War. Little or no training was given to entrenching which the experience of the Manchurian War should have taught them.

One of the units assembling in Lyndhurst was 1st Battalion of the Royal Welch Fusiliers (1/RWF). They had been stationed in Malta on the outbreak of war. They would fight alongside 1/LG defending Zandvoorde in a few short weeks as would the 2nd Battalion Scots Guards.

The Commanding Officer of 1/RWF Lieutenant Colonel Cadogan

'wasted no time in starting hard training for his battalion: exercises, weapon practice and route marches. One footsore soldier recorded he marched 300 miles round the New Forest, but there was still enough energy for the sleepy main street of Lyndhurst to be disturbed by a brawl between the Fusiliers and the Gordon Highlanders. The town's three policemen sensibly kept their distance.'

There were restrictions placed on the thousands of thirsty soldiers camped at Lyndhurst. On 9 September the following order was issued: 'All Public Houses in the neighbourhood of LYNDHURST are placed out of bounds to the troopers (sic) of the 7th Division.' Two days later the following order was issued which gives credit to the resourcefulness and enterprise of the British Tommy: 'SOUTHAMPTON is placed out of bounds to all troops of the Division.'

1st Battalion, Royal Welch Fusiliers at Lyndhurst October 1914
Rowland - extreme left, bottom row; Cadogan - sixth left;
Dooner - 7th left; Parker - 2nd right, top row;
Wodehouse - 3rd left; Poole - 8th left; Evans - 10th left.

(*Museum of the Royal Welch Fusiliers*)

The 2nd Battalion Scots Guards arrive at Lyndhurst Camp from their base at the Tower of London. (*Imperial War Museum*)

When the 7th Division deployed to Belgium they fielded 400 officers and 12,000 men. By the end of the year there were only 44 officers and 2,336 men. Back in London the effort to integrate the reservists into 1/LG at Knightsbridge Barracks

'met with little success. Tattersall's and Ward's Yard were acquired for additional stabling and men's quarters. The whole transport camped in Hyde Park. This distribution of groups here and there, with strings of public houses as connecting links, did not tend to improve our prospects.'

The utter futility of the whole business was soon realized and at the end of August 1/LG left their Knightsbridge Barracks and entrained at Nine Elms Railway Station at Battersea, London for their journey to Windmill Hill Camp outside Ludgershall, Wiltshire. Along with 2/LG and the RHG these Regiments formed the 7th Cavalry Brigade, along with K Battery Royal Horse Artillery, a signal troop and a field ambulance unit.

For thousands of loved ones an embrace on a railway platform would be the last time they saw their husband, father or brother. (*Christina Broom*)

Tending to horses at Windmill Hill Camp near Ludgershall. (*Christina Broom*)

Camping at Windmill Hill for over a month gave the regiment a chance to assimilate the reservists:

> 'Tom Phillips became one of our new Sergeant-Majors, and he at once set about restoring and maintaining order by getting in among the toughs in person and throwing his jacket off when he considered it necessary. He gave one or two a sound hiding. The result was a complete success, and the men soon held him in profound admiration and respect.'

As 1/LG was getting into shape in England, across the Channel the massive German Army was already steamrollering across Belgium and into France.

Lord Worsley wrote to his father, 4th Earl of Yarborough, from Ludgershall,

Lieutenant Hon. Gerry Ward MVO son of Lord Dudley at Windmill Hill Camp, Ludgershall in August 1914 was a troop leader in C Squadron 1/LG. (*Christina Broom*)

Lord Hugh wearing riding boots with spurs on the right. These boots would have been impractical in muddy trenches. His fellow officer is wearing ankle boots and cloth strips known as 'puttees'. We know from Lord Hugh's last letters home that he adopted puttees. Lord Hugh is also wearing a wrist watch. The change from gentlemen carrying a fob watch in their pocket to wearing one on their wrist happened during the First World War. (*Private Collection*)

'I can assure you when it comes to my turn I shall do my very best. The parting is always the worst job, and naturally I should like to see you and Mother before going, though I doubt if I shall, as you will find it very difficult to get up here. I don't want you and Mother to worry more than necessary. One naturally cannot avoid being anxious, but one must try and realise that whatever happens it is the will of God, in whose hands we all are. We can only trust in Him. That is one's greatest consolation. In case I don't see you and Mother again before going – which we don't expect to do for a week or ten days at earliest – au revoir, and God bless you both and my brothers as well. We shall hope to come back though.'

Chapter 4

The Imperial German Army

The German strategy to defeat the Belgians and the French was based on the Schlieffen plan which entailed a rapid advance through Belgium and to sweep around Paris in a bold and massive right hook. The plan had been devised more than two decades before the start of the First World War. Speed was of the essence. Any holdup to the German advance would stall the whole plan and lead to a stalemate situation. This stalemate manifested itself in years of costly trench warfare.

The assumption made by French and British strategists was that if Germany attacked France it would do so across the common Franco-German border. The BEF would assemble in the area of Le Cateau and Mauberge as a token force to bolster the French Army's left flank. In the unlikely event of the German Army smashing its way through neutral Belgium it would put the meagre BEF directly in the path of the German onslaught. This is exactly what happened. The German forces had prepared for a swift advance to victory with seemingly limitless reserves of manpower.

In the first months their tactics were probes by cavalry, often Prussian lancers called Uhlans, to establish where the allied forces were, followed by a sharp artillery barrage and then massed infantry assault. Many of these infantry assaults were columns of grey clad infantry advancing *en masse*, shoulder to shoulder. The waste of young men by the German high command was prodigious. Contemporary accounts of German attacks compared them with a crowd leaving a football match:

'Shoulder to shoulder they advanced in the same way as their ancestors fought under Frederick the Great, and, though for spectacular purposes at Grand Manoeuvres their mass formations were very effective, in actual warfare against modern weapons they proved to be a costly failure.'

The German infantry tactics at the start of the war were crude: 'The infantry company, its men, non-commissioned officers and officers were trained to function as a monolithic unit.' The view from the outset of the conflict was that the British soldiers were better than their German counterparts. This idea was supported by Morgan Crofton:

> 'It is difficult to call their infantry contemptible for they come on blindly and hopelessly to certain death. They seem to expect it and they certainly get it, but there is not a soldier in this army that does count himself as worth four Germans. The German attack forms a target that up to now has been the Gunner's Dream.'

Consequently the loss of life was on an industrial scale. Casualties suffered by the German Army at Langemarck near Ypres became known as *'Kindermorden von Ypren'* – the slaughter of the innocents.

A first-hand account from an infantry officer at the time gives an idea of what it was like facing a massed German attack:

> 'The Germans launch a strong counter-attack ... they come on bravely, surging forward in mass formation, scores of them being shot down ... the German pour a terrific fire of all arms into us. Our numbers diminish but we hang on grimly, digging ourselves farther and farther into the ground, until the whole of our bodies are under cover of mother earth. By this time I have only about twenty men left unwounded, and ammunition is running short ... I order the men to get all the ammunition they can from the dead and wounded, as there is no other method of getting a fresh supply. At the same time, I myself acquire a rifle in exchange for my sword, which I discard in order to camouflage myself as much as possible. We have learnt by this time how good the Germans are at picking out the officers.'

In fact the difficulty defenders faced was shooting the advancing Germans attackers down rapidly enough to prevent being overrun. Also the rate at which rapid fire consumed ammunition was alarming. The above account of an attack early in the war caused soldiers to search their own dead and wounded comrades for ammunition. The importance of ensuring soldiers had sufficient ammunition was learnt early on. A manual published later stated:

> 'If incapacitated ... the soldier's first duty is to place his ammunition in a conspicuous place, ready to be picked by other men, and all ranks must seize opportunities that offer for replenishing their ammunition in this manner.'

The German infantry had similar problems of ammunition supply:

> 'All units must accept a policy of *notbeheife* (makeshift). The dead and wounded ... were a perpetual source of ordnance supply.'

The German infantry advanced in massed ranks because of the training they received:

> 'It was clear to all officers who had been under fire that many men were frightened by bullets and Shrapnel and some would always be prone to run away. In company formation this was impossible; the company sergeant-major was positioned left or right flank rear so that movement out of the ranks was instantly seen by him. It was recognized that a company, still more a battalion in close formation was a dense target and more vulnerable to a single Shrapnel burst than one dispersed but none had yet experienced the intense fire which became the rule in the twentieth century.'

Also before machine guns were fully exploited the shock effect of 200 rifles of a massed company was a battle-winner – at least it was in the nineteenth century.

Many of the German units thrown into the attack in the First Battle of Ypres in October consisted of volunteers who had answered the call to arms only in August. Many of these recruits were students who were fired with patriotic zeal. The limited amount of time available to provide them with adequate training in musketry and field-craft was one of the reasons they attacked in massed formations. There simply was not enough time to train them in anything more advanced.

As the war ground on the German military learnt the lessons of the folly of massed assaults quickly and adopted specially selected and trained assault forces, or Stormtroops, which were employed successfully at the Battle of Cambrai in 1917. These innovative tactics were 'noted by junior officers in the German Army at the time notably Erwin Rommel and Heinz Guderian', who would lead *Blitzkreig* (Lightning War) assaults in the Second World War.

A novel type of infantry assault tactic was developing:

'The harsh campaigning experience … was leading regimental officers and men to cast aside the rigid tactics taught to them on the manoeuvre grounds … As the range shortened and the enemy's fire grew more intense they no longer persisted *en masse*. Ranks broke for cover. At once, the officers and non-commissioned officers began to form ad hoc assault groups to stalk the enemy trenches … The German infantry were coming to see that, in contrast to the time-honoured mass assault, the operation of numerous small groups of aggressive, determined men achieved often significant results at a low cost in casualties. It was an art which the Germans were to become accomplished.'

The German Army in 1914 was a huge organization with masses of manpower. What they lacked was time to train their troops in more sophisticated tactics than the human wave assault.

Chapter 5

Sleepwalking into War

Europe in 1914 was divided into two imperial power blocs, Britain, France and Russia against Germany and Austro-Hungary. Each country was linked together in diplomatic and military alliances like mountain climbers roped to each other. The rationale was that both sides were so colossal the prospect of war would be unthinkable. However, just like the climbers, once one fell over the edge the others were dragged after them into the abyss of war. All it would take for this tinderbox to ignite was a spark.

On 28 June 1914 Archduke Franz Ferdinand of Austria and his wife, Sophie, Duchess of Hohenberg, were assassinated by Gavrilo Princip, a Bosnian Serb, in Sarajevo. In the days and weeks that followed countries started to implement their mobilization plans and the world stumbled, unwilling or unable to stop, into its first global conflict. European capitals witnessed euphoric scenes as a wave of popular public sentiment caused thousands of people to celebrate in the streets. The general feeling across Europe was that war would be a positive experience, last a brief length of time and that their own country would benefit from it in territory or influence. These feelings were to prove tragically wrong.

On 4 August Great Britain declared war on Germany and the BEF, under the command of Sir John French, headed to mainland Europe to support their French and Belgian allies. The Secretary of State for War, Lord Kitchener, issued a typically patriotic message to all members of the BEF ending with: 'Do your duty bravely. Fear God. Honour the King.'

The message sent by His Majesty King George V to the BEF on 12 August contained the words:

'I have implicit confidence in you my soldiers. Duty is your watchword, and I know your duty will be nobly done.'

In contrast to the enthusiasm of the top brass the declaration of war was received sanguinely by a soldier in 1/LG at the Hyde Park Barracks:

'In the regiment we received the news calmly. War was our business, our calling; and the latest move simply meant business. We saw no glamour or romance in warfare. The things that mattered now were a stout horse, a serviceable rifle and ammunition, and a leader who was not a born fool. Plenty of hustle there certainly was; but it was devoid of noise and excitement.'

Other regular soldiers took the news of the declaration of war in a similarly stoic fashion:

'The men's bayonets have been sharpened; so has my sword. Who knows? It may come in handy for carving the sausages.'

Chapter 6

Mons to the Marne

By 23 August the first contact was made between British and German cavalry outside Mons in Belgium. Shortly afterwards a desperate struggle to hold Mons was conducted which is exemplified by the defence of the Nimy Bridge in the town by Lieutenant Maurice James Dease of the Royal Fusiliers. Despite his multiple wounds Lieutenant Dease kept the German advance at bay with his machine-gun platoon. The action was to win Maurice the first Victoria Cross of the First World War – and cost him his life. Also manning the machine gun was Private Sidney Godley who was wounded and also awarded the Victoria Cross for his bravery.

Lieutenant Maurice Dease, V.C.
(*Royal Fusiliers*)

This style of deployment of machine guns was, however, criticized as a tactical error:

'Machine guns were, in the majority of cases wrongly employed at the outbreak of war. They were continually pushed forward, often, into impossible places, generally against the advice of the expert (the machine-gun section commander) where they were at once spotted and just as quickly blown out of existence by opposing artillery …

machine guns were actively hampered in that duty to support the most forward infantry, by being deployed in the midst of these very troops.'

Such tactical deployment of machine guns might have been one factor in the loss of the Zandvoorde ridge.

On the following day nearby at Elouges the 1st Battalion of the Cheshire Regiment (1/Cheshire), part of 15th Brigade, was overrun by massed waves of German infantry. No fewer than four German Regiments (each of three Battalions) were actively employed to surround the 1/Cheshire position. It is noteworthy that a senior German officer, when checking the shoulder titles of the dead and wounded later said: 'I have captured a brigade, yet I find nothing but Cheshires.' It appeared that a single battalion of British 'Tommies' put up such a fight that the enemy believed they were fighting a brigade of four battalions. Later, in Zandvoorde, the Household Cavalry were also to prove that British soldiers regularly punch above their weight.

After the battle at Elouges the Commanding Officer, Colonel Boger wrote:

'We had no chance, no information and no instructions, except to guard the road and think we did all possible. I hear Jones tho' wounded, refused to surrender and pointed his revolver at them. They shot him … but buried him with military honours and a speech was made at his grave. A very gallant man.'

The Officer Commanding D Company 1/Cheshire, Captain Rae Jones, had been surrounded and could presumably have surrendered but was promptly killed after aiming his handgun at the Germans. This was obviously considered a brave act by friend and foe alike.

The diary of Major General Edward Gleichen recounts the desperate battles fought by the 1st Battalions of the Cheshire, Dorset, Bedford and Norfolk Regiments which comprised the 15th Infantry Brigade. Writing after the encounter Gleichen said of 1/Cheshire:

'The Battalion behaved magnificently in the face of terrible odds and immense difficulties. One could not expect more of them; they did their duty, and did it thunderingly well, as I should always have expected from such a gallant battalion, and I am only too grieved that they had such frightful losses.'

It is obvious that from Lord Kitchener through to individual soldiers that 'doing one's duty' often translated into sacrificing their own life. Similar actions, such as at Elouges, were taking place in the Mons area and the BEF was forced to withdraw southwards to keep in line with their French allies. This withdrawal of some 200 miles from Mons to the Marne saw notable rearguard actions.

The BEF consisted of I Corps under Sir Douglas Haig and II Corps under Sir Horace Smith-Dorrien. Both Corps, about 40,000 men each, were withdrawing from Mons on parallel courses about 10 miles apart. With the German First Army under von Kluck skirmishing with his troops in Le Cateau Smith-Dorrien addressed his commanders: 'Gentlemen, we will stand and fight.' On 26 August 1914 II Corps (half of the exhausted BEF) took on the advancing German Army at Le Cateau. As a result of a diehard attitude several battalions effectively ceased to exist as they fought to their last man.

A squadron of British lancers during the retreat from Mons. (*Imperial War Museum*)

On 27 August at Etreux the 2nd Battalion of the Royal Munster Fusiliers had a last stand and were almost wiped out. The battalion fought for almost 12 hours against nine German battalions and four artillery batteries. The only survivors were a handful of fusiliers from two platoons. In recognition of the bravery shown by the Munsters the survivors were allowed to bury their dead with respect.

On 1 September the Guards Brigade fought a heroic last stand at Villiers-Cottrets and the 1st Cavalry Brigade was also in a rearguard action at Néry where L Battery Royal Horse Artillery won three Victoria Crosses.

These actions were typical of the dogged determination of the regular British Army of the time. The thought of throwing in the towel and surrendering was anathema to them. Whilst the BEF were withdrawing southwards gallant attempts were being made to stop the Germans in their tracks elsewhere in Belgium. On 27 August Commander Samson RN arrived in Ostend which was being defended by a detachment of Royal Marines and supported by a few Royal Naval Air Service (RNAS) aeroplanes.

The First Sea Lord, Winston Churchill, dispatched two brigades from the Royal Naval Division to help the Belgian Army defend the port of Antwerp. The effort was in vain as the city was lost to the advancing Germans and the Governor of Antwerp surrendered on 10 October. 57 British sailors were killed, 138 wounded and hundreds taken prisoner by the Germans or interned for the duration of the war when they crossed into the Netherlands which was a neutral country.

The battle for Antwerp had bought precious time and the British IV Corps (consisting of the 7th Division and the 3rd Cavalry Division) needed this time to travel from England to Belgium to hold the line and try to stem the German advance.

In November the redoubtable Commander Samson was at Begersberg. This time he was in charge of a

'long naval gun mounted on a railway truck. An engine and three or four wagons completed his train. This puff-puffed up and down a stretch of railway and shelled concentration areas behind the German lines. Samson had an aeroplane and did his own 'spotting' in it.'

Chapter 7

Race to the Sea

Between 5th and 12th September the French Army and the BEF were able to defeat the German Army at the Battle of the Marne and start pushing them back northwards. This was a war of manoeuvre as each side tried to outflank each other and it became crucial to stretch the frontline to the North Sea. Once the 'Race to the Sea' finished the frontline stabilized and led to four years of trench warfare. The Germans and the Allies extended their frontlines towards the Channel coast. In this venture the Allies had too much line to defend with too few troops and no reinforcements on the horizon.

As the decimated BEF (plus III Corps) arrived at the Aisne, IV Corps were heading southwards from Zeebrugge. Ultimately they would have their rendezvous with destiny near Ypres. Desperate times call for desperate measures and although the British cavalry brigades were used initially in their traditional role, necessity required them to plug the gaps in the line by manning trenches which would normally have been done by infantry battalions. This was the exact fate of the Household Cavalry and Lord Hugh. Once at the River Aisne the Germans realized that if they could attack successfully in the north on a line from Ypres towards Calais they could take the Channel Ports and cut off the British or swing around to the south and take Paris – or both. That was von Fabeck's intention and he left no doubt about his determination to smash the British line when he circulated his orders stressing that

'The breakthrough will be of decisive importance. We must and will therefore conquer, settle forever the centuries-long struggle against our most detested enemy. We will finish with the British … and other trash, feeble adversaries.'

IV Corps, plus French and Belgian units, were strung out southwards across Belgium in a thin screen of infantry and cavalry units attempting to join up with I Corps which was moving up from the Aisne in the face of increasing German military might. By 14 October the 7th Division reached a position a few miles south east of Ypres and joined up with Allenby's Cavalry Corps from the BEF. Only a week later did I Corps infantry Battalions start to appear to supplement the tenuous positions held by a thin line of cavalrymen in shallow makeshift trenches.

Mounting pressure from the Germans, as well as British losses, caused a series of hasty reshuffles to hold the line. Having advanced from the Marne the main part of the British Army found itself sandwiched on the Aisne between the French Fifth and Sixth Armies as they faced the Germans. It was decided to move their force to the left wing of the French thereby blocking the enemy's route to the Channel ports and making their own supply lines shorter. For the British there was the inviting prospect of leaving the trenches along the Aisne River and a return to more open warfare across Flanders. Their high command did not believe that the German Army had enough manpower to hold the frontline from Switzerland all the way to the North Sea so decided to attack towards Bethune and outflank the Germans.

On 18 October Sir John French gave the order to 'advance and engage the enemy wherever met', as he thought that the German forces were over stretched and could be pushed back. French did not know that the Germans had plans of their own. Thousands of fresh soldiers from the German Fourth Army were arriving in Brussels and Ghent intent on driving headlong through the British and on to Calais. A head-on clash between the Germans and the British was only a matter of time.

On 4 October the 7th Division set off for Southampton docks to embark for the Continent. Initially they were destined to make the relatively short Channel crossing to Boulogne, but as the military situation deteriorated it was decided to land at Zeebrugge instead. The Royal Navy had to find escort vessels to protect the convoy which inevitably led to a delay.

The War Office ordered General Capper to disembark at Zeebrugge with a view to assisting and supporting the Belgian Army defending Antwerp. However Lord Kitchener instructed Capper not to take undue risks and not to get his Division bogged down and trapped in the city. Kitchener knew

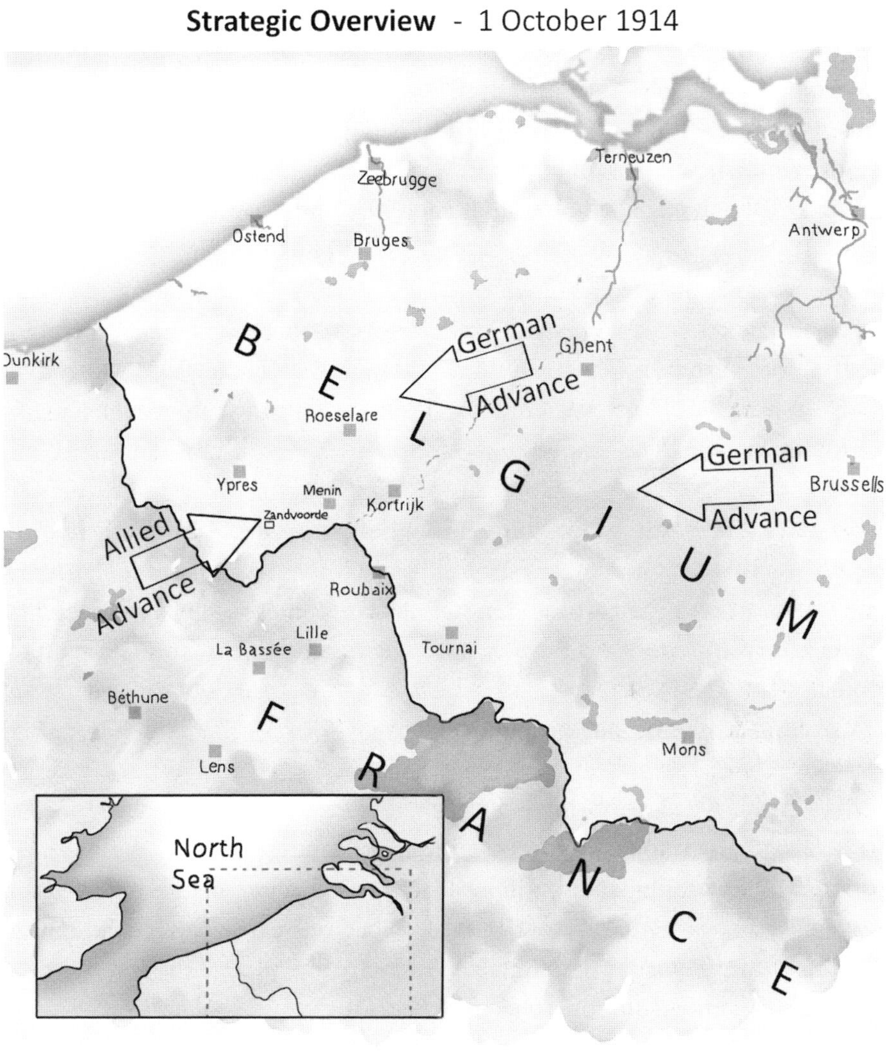

Strategic Overview - 1 October 1914

Map 1: The Allied Advance indicates the British intention to outflank the German Army. The opposing arrows indicate the 4th German Army's line of attack to strike towards the Channel ports.

that Antwerp was a lost cause. Fresh orders from Sir Henry Rawlinson instructed the 7th Division to head for Ghent and Ypres.

It was a confusing time – with ambiguous orders and insufficient information upon which to make strategic decisions. IV Corps were lucky not to have got drawn into the forlorn hope of defending Antwerp.

Whereas the 7th Division had embarked at Southampton after leaving their Lyndhurst assembly area on 4 October, the 3rd Cavalry Division (consisting of the 6th and 7th Cavalry Brigades) followed a couple of days later to complete the IV Corps after travelling by train from Windmill Hill Camp, Ludgershall in Wiltshire.

Lord Worsley managed to write home,

'We were recalled from weekend leave yesterday – as a precaution. We expect however to receive orders to move tomorrow, so I write now to say au revoir and wish you luck. Take care of yourself and Mother. Keep her busy. Her contributions of aspirin and chocolate will be most useful … God bless you both.'

On 6 October Lord Hugh and his C Squadron 1/LG had arrived at Southampton ready to embark on a ship to take them across The Channel and were sent off to a nearby common following the age old policy of 'Hurry up. Get there … And wait', which would be familiar to any military man or woman.

Corporal of Horse Lloyd recalls the move:

'At last, on Sunday morning, 5 October, we were ordered to entrain at Ludgershall at 6 pm. Messages sent out to roundup all of the regiment. Incredible as it may seem, when the moment came to march out, not a man was missing. As a matter of fact, we had one extra, though nobody noticed him at the time. He was a civilian friend of one of the reservists, who, determined to go to the front with his chum, secured a suit of khaki somewhere, and passed unnoticed in the crowd.'

This 'stowaway' was a man called Tingley. He was adopted by a quartermaster Bob Harrison to help out on the supply wagons in return for food and shelter. The temptation to see some action led to Tingley picking up a rifle and joining his friends in the frontline. Almost inevitably, on 6 November 1914 he was killed. (6361 Private Frederick Sylven Tingley of D Squadron 1st (King's) Dragoon Guards; his name is engraved on the Ypres (Menin Gate) Memorial.)

Lloyd continued –

'A short journey of a couple of hours brought us to Southampton. To the accompaniment of much lurid language, horses were detrained and we mounted and formed up. Then began what threatened to become an endless promenade of the outskirts of the town. At long last we turned up on the Common. Horses were pegged down on ground-lines, after which we bivouacked beside them. I rolled myself up in a blanket, stuck my head in the saddle, and slept through the remainder of the night in fits and starts.'

Lord Hugh's letter to his wife read:

'My Own Darling, Much to our annoyance last night we arrived at the docks we were sent on here and arrived in the dark but pegged down at night. We bivouacked close to the horses. I wonder where we are going it looks rather like Belgium but one can't tell … I think we are going over in small boats. 1 Squadron in each. It will be a relief when we get over.'

The hurried nature of Lord Hugh's departure is indicated by the fact that the letter mentions sending three keys back to Lady Grosvenor including his house key and even one to the Knightsbridge Barracks in Hyde Park!

In August there was a popular feeling that the war would be 'over by Christmas' which led to a massive surge of young men to join up before it was too late. By October though, Lord Hugh and his comrades would have been under no illusion that the hostilities would be concluded swiftly or easily. They would have heard the accounts of heroic actions from the Mons to the Marne. Lord Hugh and his men knew what they were up against.

According to the official history:

'The cavalry had not commenced embarking at Southampton until 10 am on the 7th owing to the ships not being ready, and only after a five hours wait at Dover, had it been conveyed across to Ostend, where it began to arrive about 4 am on the 8th. Four ships, apparently picked at hazard for they contained parts of several different units, were taken, however, to Zeebrugge.'

Later that day Lord Hugh left England never to return. His next letter home was written on board the SS *Algerian* later that evening:

'My Darling, We are all safely on board I had to send St George and his troop to another ship as there was no room for him a great bore but it couldn't be helped as we have the Headquarters of 6th Brigade with us General Makins and staff including Charlie Fitzmaurice and de Karoop. This is an awful old tub 3000 tons at the most and we are frightfully cramped.'

Of those temporary shipmates Lord Hugh mentions: 'St George' was Second Lieutenant H. St. George (killed in action); 'Makins' was Brigadier General Sir Ernest Makins a veteran of the Anglo-Boer War who after the First World War was elected MP for Knutsford in Cheshire from 1922 to 1945; and 'Fitzmaurice' was Lord Charles Petty-Fitzmaurice (killed in action). The 'awful old tub' the SS *Algerian* was herself to become a casualty of war when she struck a German mine and sank near Cowes on 12 January 1916.

Conditions on board these makeshift troopships were chaotic and crowded; the cabin Morgan Crofton used was described as 'like a monkey house'. The troops out on the open deck suffered worse:

'Everything went well till we got out into the open Channel and the breeze freshened up … There was nothing else for it … find a sheltered corner where we kept falling off to sleep as we stood up, and spent our waking moments cursing the cold, the ship, and everything we could think of.'

The relief at finally embarking for operations was obvious as Lord Hugh went on to write: 'Close Brooks and I have taken the Doctor's cabin as he has not turned up. Gerry, Brocklehurst, Kelly and interpreter have all found places. I believe we sail at 1am and I think our destination is somewhere about Ostend I don't know for certain but there is not much doubt about it. It looks as if we are going to have a dash at the German lines of communications grand fun! We may land possibly North of Ostend and it looks as if we might have some pretty good hunting as long as the horses last out.'

'Close Brooks' was Lieutenant J. C. Close Brooks; 'Gerry' was the Honourable Lieutenant Gerald Francis Ward M.V.O.; 'Kelly' was probably Captain Edward Dennis Festus Kelly. All three men were to die with Lord Hugh. 'Brocklehurst' was Lieutenant Sir Phillip Brocklehurst, Bart. who, although wounded, survived the war. It seems that Lord Hugh had grasped the general strategic situation. At the time the allies thought the German armies were stretched too thinly leaving their right flank exposed. If the British cavalry could be deployed to strike the enemy from the side, along their 'lines of communication', it would deal them a devastating blow. As a cavalryman Lord Hugh was enthusiastic for this opportunity to show what his squadron could do.

In fact thousands of Germans of their 4th Army were getting ready to launch a new offensive, not southward again towards Paris, but west straight for the Channel ports to eliminate the BEF. The official British history records:

Soldiers from the 7th Division were deployed to Ostend to cover the disembarkation of the 3rd Cavalry Division. (*Imperial War Museum*)

'In view of the information that strong German forces were advancing from Lille, the 7th Division, on 8 October marched from Bruges and Ostend and formed on an arc of a circle four miles outside the town to cover the landing of the 3rd Cavalry Division.'

Although the 3rd Cavalry Division arrived offshore of Ostend on the evening of 7 October they had to wait until the following day to disembark as the Belgian harbours were packed with transport shipping.

On 8 October Lord Hugh was getting ready to disembark from SS *Algerian* off the Belgian coast and managed to write another hurried letter home:

'My Darling, All well so far. We arrived off here in the middle of the night and expect to disembark soon about 11am. We lay off Deal for a long time waiting for instructions and a pilot. It was a lovely sight seeing all the ships lighting up and 12 destroyers rushing out as our escorts.'

Security was becoming a concern as Lord Hugh went on:

'This will escape the censors but don't say too much about where we are. I don't want to get into trouble. I hear they shot 2 German spies in Ostend yesterday so I expect there are several left. The Germans don't leave much to chance.'

Lord Hugh also appreciated that the Allies needed all available help to stop the relentless German advance by repeating the story that:

'I believe the Indian Troops are here now but no one knows much.'

These 'Indian Troops' were the Indian Expeditionary Force sent to support the British. It consisted of two Cavalry Divisions of the Indian Army as well as the 3rd (Lahore) Division and the 7th (Meerut) Division. They landed in Marseille in mid–October before serving with distinction on the Western Front.

When the 3rd Cavalry Division finally disembarked on 8 October they were greeted enthusiastically by the Belgian population with the official 1/LG war diary stating that they

'disembarked and remained awaiting orders on the quay till 3.30 pm then marched slowly through Blankenberghe the column was considerably delayed in the streets of the town owing to the non-receipt of orders. This was unfortunate as it led to the ranks being considerably broken by inhabitants offering hospitality. It seems undesirable for troops to remain halted in friendly towns.'

The friendly reception given to the troops was also recorded by Morgan Crofton:

'Given a Chrysanthemum by a small girl in the street, and shook hands with several unknown persons in various stages of cleanliness!'

At the quayside one Life Guardsman noted that

'several civilians came alongside as we were awaiting orders to disembark, and tried to converse with us in broken English. They got little information, as the troops refused to discuss anything beyond the prospects of getting something to drink.'

On the following day, 9 October, the Belgian city of Antwerp fell to the German Army. This released thousands of German soldiers to join the advance westwards. Another of the repercussions of the fall of Antwerp was that IV Corps, comprising the 7th Division and the 3rd Cavalry Division, under Lieutenant General Sir Henry Rawlinson which had originally been earmarked to defend the city were now transferred to Sir John French's command. With IV Corps arrival at Ypres French gained a sense of optimism:

'Not only was a defended line established by the Allies to the sea but, a matter of great satisfaction to Sir John, the British Expeditionary Force was concentrating fast under his hand for a second excursion into Belgium. But this time he was far stronger than he had been when he had taken them forward to Mons. The Germans, he believed, were weaker; perhaps close to the end of their resources.'

By 10 October the cavalry had been accommodated in a Belgian chateau. According to the Life Guards' war diary:

'Reached destination orders then received to go into billets at Ruddervoorde. On reaching this place it was found to be crowded with Belgian troops, so Regiment bivouacked 1½ M S of village at the Chateau at 6 pm.'

The exact location of the chateau is not known – it was possibly in the Rapenburg Kast or Kast Lakebos area or Munken Kasteel.

The Daily Graphic reported:

'Messages from Berlin received here state that the French attempt to outflank the German right wing may be considered definitely to have failed and that the Germans are now even menacing the French and British left wing with outflanking movements.'

On the following day Lord Hugh wrote home from the chateau:

'My Darling, Well we are all very well and fit so far. I have had no fighting yet but we are getting closer every day to the Germans. We are at present billeted in the grounds of a very pretty chateau. My squadron is in the garden under the windows. The mess the horses make is awful but everyone seems pleased to see us. It sounds very comfortable but unfortunately the Headquarters of the Brigade and the Headquarters of the Regt got into the house and there was no room for any of us.'

This letter was the first to receive a stamp PASSED BY CENSOR as all post was scrutinised to ensure confidential information was not being sent home by the troops. Lord Hugh's compassion for his soldiers came across in this letter:

Corporal Major
Phillips on the right.
(*Christina Broom*)

'So far I have lost Corporal Major Phillips his horse fell and broke a
bone in his ankle he is a great loss. Will you let his wife know. We hope
he will soon be right.'

Corporal Major Phillips had been credited with maintaining order amongst
the unruly reservists back at Windmill Hill. Losses of experienced non-
commissioned officers such as Tom Phillips must have been difficult to bear.

Lord Hugh had to put down a horse which had a contagious disease called 'strangles' which, at that time, was incurable.

Lord Hugh alluded to the reconnaissance role which the cavalry were engaged in:

> 'Harold's squadron has started off on reconnaissance with two armoured motors. We are waiting until we hear news before we move.'

The 'armoured motors' were likely to be from the Royal Navy Air Service (RNAS) which was under the direction of the First Lord of the Admiralty, Sir Winston Churchill. These Rolls-Royce cars were modified by welding armour plate to their sides and mounting a machine-gun on them. They were the forerunner of the modern armoured fighting vehicle.

Lord Hugh wrote:

> 'Ned's friend Commander Samson has been buzzing about in his armoured motor this morning with a huge gun, he is a splendid man and puts the fear of God into the old Germans.'

Commander Samson was a pioneering aviator and obviously acquainted with Ned Grosvenor. Lord Hugh's younger brother Lord Edward 'Ned' Grosvenor was in the Royal Flying Corps and had also served in the Royal Naval Air Service. The primary purpose of the RNAS armoured cars was to rescue pilots downed behind enemy lines.

On the following day, 11 October, the British Cavalry were in action at Hazebrouck.

By 12 October Lord Hugh's Squadron suffered its first battle casualty when one of his horses was shot by mistake by a Belgian unit whilst patrolling Lendelede, as his official report notes:

> 'Have occupied Lendelede and sent patrols down all roads running South in my Section – my advanced guard was fired at by a Belgian Cyclist patrol from Southern side of Lendelede, one horse hit in quarter. Belgian Officer in charge of patrol reports all clear round Courtai in the immediate vicinity. Sweveghem SE of Courtai and

Heule still in telephonic communication with Courtrai. Belgian officer also reports six armoured motors at Gheluwe' From C Squad, 1st Life Guards, Lendelede 3.5pm H Grosvenor Capt

In Lord Hugh's letter home a couple of days later he recalled:

'The first time my squadron came under fire was from a Belgian patrol luckily they are rotten shots and only killed a horse, one of the best of course. Very annoying the Belgian officer in charge of patrol wept on discovering his mistake.'

This type of so-called 'friendly fire' incident is more prevalent when the situation is fluid and soldiers are nervous. The next day Lord Hugh's men were called on to protect the Divisional Headquarters at Roulers and subsequently east of Iseghem. During this time C Squadron and other cavalry units were deployed to and fro around the Belgian countryside east of Ypres to seek out the German advance guards as well to protect other units. Lord Hugh would have travelled the road from Ypres towards Menin where his name was later to be inscribed on the Menin Gate to remember the 54,896 Commonwealth soldiers who died in the area with no known grave. At this time Ypres had a civilian population of 18,929; on the following day, 13 October, the British 3rd Cavalry Division arrived there and the German Army occupied Lille and Ghent. Heavy fighting was taking place between Bethune and La Bassée. The fatigue of operations was beginning to tell on the soldiers as a weary Life Guardsman described:

'We were too weary even to go in search of something to eat and drink. So I just sat down on the edge of the pavement with my horse's reins over my arm, and was soon fast asleep. I knew nothing more till about 5 am, while it was still dark, when I was awakened by shouts of 'Mount!' When I awoke I discovered I had been sleeping soundly in the gutter, where the stream of muddy water from the street had converted me into a waterlogged island in the middle of a small lake. My poor horse stood there like a wet rag, waiting for me.'

On entering Ypres the Life Guards were witnesses to the demise of an enemy aircraft:

'During our halt of about two hours in Ypres there was a short period of breathless excitement. A German Taube flew over the town at a fair height. He was greeted by a burst of fire from a machine-gun which perceptibly staggered him. He did not crash, but lost height slowly and started coming down directly over the square. Civilians came rushing out of their houses with shotguns and revolvers, and finally, when he was low enough, they actually bombarded him with bricks. He was brought down over the square, so we did not see what eventually became of him, though it was not difficult to guess.'

At this stage Ypres had not been ravaged by battle. Within a month it was a very different story according to one soldier:

'We reached Ypres finally after many halts, and filed through its dark and deserted streets. The Town had been well shelled for some little time, and from the fitful flashes of our torch we could see gaunt walls and debris, the result of the shelling. There was something very eerie in our procession along the *pavé* streets, which re-echoed to our horses' feet. Not a soul appeared. It was indeed a City of the Dead.'

The political significance of Ypres from a Belgian point of view could not be overstated. It was the last Belgian town in Allied hands. King Albert of the Belgians was genuinely concerned that if this last part of his land was taken it might spell the death knell for his nation. The strategy of defending the Ypres salient was criticised late in 1914:

'The Salient at Ypres is simply an inferno. It is not war, but murder pure and simple. The massacre that is going on here is not realised at home.'

There were calls for the line to be straightened and the Salient given up. By 14 October Sir Henry Rawlinson with IV Corps had made it to Ypres.

The Cloth Hall at Ypres in 1914. (*Imperial War Museum*)

As Allenby's Cavalry Corps drew up from Bethune the 3rd Cavalry Division operated from Zonnebeke to the Foret d'Houlthurst filling the gap between the 7th Division and the French cavalry. The 7th Division pushed forwards into a crescent shape six miles east of Ypres from Zonnebeke through Kruiseik to Zandvoorde. German forces had taken Menin and cavalry lancers from the 20th Uhlan Regiment patrolled forwards in the direction of Ypres, but

'there was no question of the ground being firmly held. The occasional British armoured car patrol and the aggression of the British Cavalry made the German hold on this area extremely precarious.'

Chapter 8

Lord Hugh's First Contact

Lord Hugh's first contact with the enemy came on 14 October at the village of Gheluwe outside Menin. His official report read:

> 'We had some small engagements with Uhlans to-day. Found Gheluwe occupied by about 30 Germans, attacked dismounted with two troops and ousted them, regret to say Corporal of H Leggett killed. 10.25 pm H Grosvenor Capt.'

Corporal of Horse William Thomas Leggett was 23 years old when he was killed. He was buried at Harlebeke New British Cemetery.

Dirk Decuypere, a local of Gheluwe, saw that the Germans had entered the village earlier in the day and had posted sentries in and around the tram station. The following is what he recorded:

> 'It is close to 3 pm when Captain Grosvenor, commanding officer of C Squadron, 1st Life Guards, enters the village by way of the Dadizelestraat and is informed by civilians about the German presence. Grosvenor estimates their numbers at 30 or so. He investigates about the enemy positions and divides his Squadron in two. First phase of the attack: to steal up on the sentries as close as possible and eliminate them. A first group approaches the centre of the village through the Beselarestraat: the advance guard on foot, rifles at the ready, followed by the remainder hanging low behind the necks of the horses. A second group – about 20 – leaves all the horses behind, and cautiously follows the tram track alongside Nieuwstraat towards the convent. This track will bring them straight to the tram station: the main target of the attack. The British are silently sneaking through the ditch towards the bend where the tram lines cross the road. There, the Life Guards jump out

and swiftly cross the street, then move on across the Reutelbeke (a brook) and towards the Leperstraat. The station is just across. In the centre of the village the first British shots ring out: one of the two sentries at the Café Hert falls to the ground. Sacristan Ghesquiere hears windows smash to pieces and cautiously watches outside. At Albert Vandamme's (now the town hall) he notices a British soldier standing still while 10 other British are warily running alongside the Vrouwstraat bend so as to get into Menenstraat. A vehement 10 minutes' exchange of fire in the latter street follows shortly after. A thoughtful Life Guard who happens to meet up with scared villagers praying in the church at that moment, guides them through the sacristy door to the presbytery. Also at the station there is intensive gunfire. The Germans are totally surprised and retreat via the farm of Theophiel Ghesquiere (now Zuidstraat 430) and the houses at Vierhoeken (now Voorhoek). This is the best escape route towards Menenstraat and Menin. Corporal William Leggett is among the pursuing British Cavalrymen who reach the northerly hedge of the farm Ghesquiere when he is hit by a bullet. He spills from his horse and falls into the hedge, while his horse dashes away over the open fields.'

This seems to show that Lord Hugh had made a sound tactical appreciation and ordered a two-pronged approach. He realised that the horses would be unsuitable for fighting in a built-up area so he left most behind. However, he must have ordered some of his troopers to continue the advance mounted. This would give him the option of charging the enemy or outflanking them and cutting off their retreat. According to Dirk Decuypere's account the individual troopers seemed to be advancing tactically and were displaying the dismounted skills expected of infantrymen.

This engagement was also reported on by Reggie Wyndham:

'Hugh Grosvenor (Captain Lord Hugh Grosvenor) came up and told me that on flank patrol he had surprised about 16 Uhlans in Gheluwe. They had come from Menin by the light railway. They surprised the Germans, killed three, captured one and wounded several, but were afraid to hunt them out of the houses in case they managed to fire at his horses.'

Lord Hugh's First Contact
14 October 1914

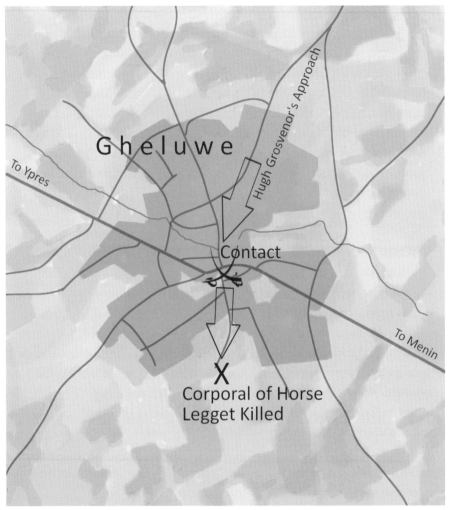

Map 2: Lord Hugh's first contact on 14 October at Gheluwe. (*David Parkland*)

Lord Hugh's account of the action to his wife read:

'Yesterday I was protecting the infantry's left flank and on my way in to join the Brigade I was told that a village in front of me was occupied by 30 Uhlans so we went for them. I dismounted 2 troops Gerry's and

Brocklehurst's and tried to round them up however they ran but we bagged 2 or 3 killed and more were wounded. I went with Gerry and had most of the fun. It was like a rat hunt in and out of houses through gardens, it was rather awkward as they separated and got into houses and behind hedges and had pots at us from unexpected directions. However we cleared the village, unluckily one of my best corporals was shot dead bullet through the head. We had just got through a gap in a fence and he was standing between Gerry and me, poor devil he didn't feel anything. We then mounted and went on Gerry carrying an Uhlan lance which he had taken when two more Uhlans appeared on foot and ran across a turnip field like 2 baboons. Gerry chased one on Bennett and took him prisoner. You would have laughed to see Gerry and Lance and Bennett pounding across the field. The other poor devil was killed.'

In Jonathan Ali's book 'Our Boys' about soldiers who died in the First World War from his village of Hawkshaw in Lancashire there is a recurring theme of letters of condolence written home by comrades, commanding officers and chaplains all claiming that the soldier in question died from a fatal gunshot wound to the head. Time and again the next of kin would be told that their loved one died instantaneously and without suffering. The number of these deaths from being shot in the head appears to be implausibly high. One conclusion was that the survivors wanted to give comfort to the bereaved families by 'gilding the lily' and made up an account of a swift and painless death as a kindness to distressed relatives in their grief. One may speculate if Lord Hugh did the same in his description of the death of Corporal of Horse Leggett to his loved ones. If so, it shows that Lord Hugh was considerate of the feelings of others.

This action occurred during the brief, but critical, open warfare phase. Such patrols were described as:

'Small bodies of men, who were usually pushed boldly out a long way in advance of the main position, not only gave that 'early information' of the enemy's movements ... but also by their bold action must have caused the enemy delay and inconvenience out of all proportion to their numerical strength.'

The road into Geluwe today from the direction of Menen. (*M. J. McBride*)

Fields on the outskirts of Geluwe towards Menen. (*M. J. McBride*)

In Lord Hugh's letter to his young son Gerald he wrote:

'Dear Gerald, Just a line to tell you I am very well and busy fighting the Germans. Tell Aunt Molly I was so pleased to get her letter and yours. Write again both of you. One of my men stuck a German with his sword the other day and we have shot several. I have picked off one or two myself, at least I think and hope so. I think Uncle Jerry from Ash is quite well, but his Battalion has been fighting hard for the last week and I can't get news of him. I hear you and John have great fun riding together. You might get a bit of hunting this winter. Give granny my best love and tell her I will write as soon as I can. It is the most lovely hot day today and we are having a rest in the sun. The Enemy's shells are bursting about ¼ mile away luckily they don't know we are peacefully writing letters here. I saw Peter Poole today very well but his Battalion lost all their officers except 3 and have only 250 men left. Give fat Pete my best love and love to Aunt Molly and Gran. Your loving Daddy.

'Aunt Molly' was Lord Hugh's sister Mary; 'Uncle Jerry' was Captain Lord Gerald Richard Grosvenor of 2nd Battalion Scots Guards who was wounded and taken prisoner-of-war on 25 October, he was the half-brother of Lord Hugh; 'Fat Pete' was a nickname given to Lord Hugh's second son who later became the 5th Duke of Westminster and 'Peter Poole' was an officer in 1/RWF. It was not until February 1915 that orders went out: 'Officers will discard their swords, revolvers and Sam Browne belts, and go in with rifles, bandoliers and bayonets.' Lord Hugh's comment that he '*picked off one or two myself*' could, however, well indicate that he had acquired a rifle to supplement his revolver and sword.

Corporal of Horse Lloyd recalls the encounter in Gheluwe. He described how one of the Uhlans was shot as he rode away:

'The second one took to running across country and was pursued by the Hon Gerald Ward and a couple of mounted men. Soon he stopped, raised his carbine, and aimed straight at the officer. As the latter rode straight at him, he changed his mind, threw the gun down, and put his hands up. A wild fellow, named Bellingham, of the 'Skins' (Inniskillen Dragoon Guards), galloped at him and ran him through the body with his sword. He then calmly wiped his sword on his horse's mane and remarked, "That's the way to serve them bastards". Those present were shocked at the cold-bloodedness of the deed.'

Whether Lord Hugh witnessed this incident or not is impossible to say; indeed the account may or not have been accurate. However it is possible that soldiers were under no illusions that surrender, if offered, would be respected. Historian Richard Holmes reflected on the practicalities of offering and accepting surrender in the heat of battle:

'Surrendering during a firefight is never an easy business. Whatever military law or international conventions may say about the matter, a rough natural justice often induces victor to finish off vanquished with a shot or a bayonet thrust, muttering "Too late, chum". The defeated soldier has a much better chance of living long enough to become a prisoner if there is an element of formality to the surrender and his own leader comes to terms with an enemy officer.'

Refusing to accept the surrender of a foe occurred on both sides in the First World War as this description of a German attack near Ypres demonstrates: 'Casualties increased, there were wounded men lying everywhere, but a boundless anger at the enemy rose within us ... with loud Hurrahs! We hurled ourselves at the enemy trenches – at which point the British, almost without exception, threw down their weapons and put their hands up. They had still been firing at us when we were barely five metres from their trenches. That had a lot to do with the fact that some British soldiers still lost their lives at the point of a bayonet.'

In the First World War soldiers on both sides did offer surrender and it was accepted, but not universally.

The German cavalry which Lord Hugh fought were the 20th (2nd Württemberg) Uhlans King William I Regiment of the Army of Württemberg. During the First World War the 20th Uhlans served as divisional cavalry for the German 26th (1st Württemberg) Division. The Uhlans were armed primarily with the lance, and were used for scouting and foraging duties for which they became notorious. The Uhlans were said to be:

'Shy of coming to close quarters, and, taking them all in all, not very likeable customers. In their methods they resembled prowling packs of wolves rather than soldiers. Each Uhlan was armed to the teeth. He carried a long straight sword, which was an extremely useful weapon, and could be used to cut as well as thrust. In addition, he carried an iron lance as long as a telegraph pole and known to our troops as a 'gas pipe'. For firearms they had an automatic pistol, and a short carbine sighted to six hundred metres.'

These soldiers were recruited from the Kingdom of Württemberg which is now known as Baden-Württemberg bordering Bavaria in the south of Germany. The German cavalry tended to work more cooperatively with their infantry than the British. Uhlans would scout ahead for their Jäger Regiments (light infantry) which were units traditionally recruited from huntsmen and foresters. Although the German cavalry was numerically superior to the British they were not considered as effective. According to a German cavalry officer:

'Owing to the advantage of long term service, as well as to the lesson learned in the South African War, the British Cavalry were indisputably far better trained for dismounted action than their Continental fellow horsemen.'

Examination of German horses by a British cavalryman showed a lack of horsemanship:

'The captured horses were reduced to skin, bone and sores. The saddlery was superior to that of our officers. The wallets were huge and contained more odds and ends than a whole troop of ours. The horses' nosebags were neither deficient or empty. No wonder the much-boosted Uhlan is a poor cavalryman. Each of them ought to have a lorry instead of an unfortunate horse. The ideal cavalry soldier travels as light as possible and is always nursing his horse.'

The overburdening of the German cavalry was also noted by Morgan Crofton:

'The German cavalry is beneath contempt. They overload their saddles so much, both fore and aft, that they can neither dismount when mounted, nor mount when dismounted.'

If the German cavalryman failed to impress his British counterpart whilst on horseback he was even less impressive when dismounted:

'The German trooper had failed to be taught the basic skills necessary for successful dismounted action. In musketry he was as feeble as the carbine with which he practised it.'

In one action on 19th October an officer of the Royals reported that,

'they shot abominably. A man in my troop kept raising his cap to the Germans saying "Third-class shots, third-class!"'

The British also had a poor opinion of the French cavalry:

'The British soldiers were intrigued to find them wearing multi-coloured jackets, sweeping cloaks, plumed helmets and, here and there, steel cuirasses. The popgun appearance of the cavalry carbines heightened an impression of comic opera.'

Sir Douglas Haig also commented on the French cavalry:

'I watched the smart dapper little fellows march off. Several had "jemima" boots, most unsuited for war and mud such as we soon encountered in Flanders … the little carbine with which they were armed was not much better than an ordinary rook rifle!'

Like all troops then and now Lord Hugh took the opportunity to ask for additional items, or 'comforts', from home in his letters. In this letter he asked:

'Will you send me some indelible pencils and cigarettes. I changed my clothes today for the first time since we left home so I have plenty of them for the moment.'

Lord Hugh did bump into his namesake and half nephew Hugh Richard Arthur Grosvenor, 'Bendor', the 2nd Duke of Westminster. In Lord Hugh's letter he stated: 'Bendor I have seen twice looking very fit.'

At this stage in the war Bendor was a liaison officer on French's staff using his own Rolls Royce driven by his chauffeur from the Eaton Estate, George Powell.

Lord Hugh kept cheerful and had an optimistic bias:

'I hope to see Harry and others soon. One doesn't hear much news but the little I do hear sounds good and everyone seems pleased. This is a scrap as we are standing by ready to move. All my Squadron officers doing well. St George is a ripper. Always cheery and never perturbed. Gerry working like a black and always turns up in the evening with

Painting of the 2nd Duke of Westminster 'Bendor' by John Lavery. (*Private collection*)

something to eat in his pocket so we are a very happy party, we have got a funny old man as an interpreter attached to us he can't talk as much French as I can but he is a nice old thing and we all rag him and send him foraging for food. It now looks as if we are going to have an easy day at last and we do want one badly. We have had funny places to sleep in lately frequently in the open and nearly always more or less on outposts. It has been an anxious time for the Supreme Commanders but now they are happy again. You will have to read between the lines here the censorship is awfully strict. I saw Peter Cookson for a moment yesterday looking fat and flourishing. HH gets very excited but luckily we have an excellent man called Kearsey attached he quietens things down and luckily his advice is taken. One gets tired of the sound of guns they boom away from morning to night. Close Brooks and St George wish me to thank you for bothering over their affairs. Bless you Darling. Give my love to Mummy and Moll and Nell and tell them to write. Love to the boys. My writing paper is packed on the wagon so I have to use this. Tell Nell her horses are well so far but Goliath died suddenly must have poisoned himself. Your Own Hugh'

'Harry' was possibly Henry George Grosvenor (1864–1914) half-brother of Lord Hugh; 'HH' was possibly Lieutenant-Colonel His Highness Duke of Teck and 'Kearsey' was probably Captain A. Kearsey, Brigade-Major, 7th Cavalry Brigade. Lord Hugh mentions an interpreter in his letters. The provision of interpreters for the army was an experiment which failed. In December 1914 they were withdrawn as:

> 'Many have merely been a nuisance, for the majority of them are too old for subordinate rank, and also, never having done any soldiering, are usually hopelessly at sea. Some of them too were bad linguists, so there was little to justify their existence.'

On the same day the Germans occupied Bruges and Ghent. The German commander Falkenhayn ordered the four fresh Corps of raw, eager young soldiers to hold their position for a few days. A screen of German cavalry would veil their intention to hurl the Corps against the Allies who were 'pre-occupied with the business of concentrating and reorganising. The aim of this operation was to seize one splendid consolation prize in 1914: Calais.'

In Lord Hugh's letter home on 15 October the strain of constant operational duties was having a detrimental effect on men and horses:

'My Darling, Just got your letter. I haven't had a moment to write lately as we have been trekking about all the time always saddled up before dawn and always getting into bivouac or billets after dark, the horses are getting very thin and we are short of sleep, but very well.'

Trekking was an interesting and germane word for Lord Hugh to use as it could well describe the type of operations used by the Boer Kommandos which many of his troopers would have been familiar with from their service in South Africa. The condition of the horses was mentioned by Lord Hugh and it must have been distressing to all of the horsemen to see how their mounts suffered.

Morgan Crofton described the plight of the horses in pitiful detail:

'The horses stand about all over the place looking miserable. They have had no hay for a month and they gnaw everything that they can get hold of. There is not a tree which has not had its bark gnawed off as high as a horse can reach, and a wagon stands just outside our door which is half eaten by them, one side entirely and half the other … On mobilization we had 400 or so requisitioned horses sent to us, which had come from every kind of home. Many were 100 guinea hunters and coach horses belonging to people like Vanderbilt and other rich men, and these animals had lived in well warmed stables, with masses of good food and straw for their bedding. For weeks now they were always in the open, tied up all day and night to trees and hedges, and owing to every man being required in the trenches, only a few could be spared to look after 20 or 30 each.'

Men were not the only casualties of war as described in this account from the Clarke Papers in the Liddle Collection:

'We were often hungry and so were the mules and horses – and how those poor creatures suffered … Innocent victims of man-made madness. They broke your heart, especially when you passed the injured ones, left to die, in agony and screaming with pain and terror.'

It was also common amongst British troops to try and pass messages to their loved ones of their location in code in their letters to evade censorship. So, for example, soldiers operating near the French town of Albert on The Somme would often write: 'I have seen lots of Albert recently'. Lord Hugh appears to have tried to let his wife know where he was with the following cryptic sentence: *'Edgar Saw Wombat Yesterday you can judge from that more or less where we are now.'* This is a baffling sentence. It remains a mystery if it was an anagram, or points of the compass or nicknames of comrades (or their horses). Whatever the meaning Lord Hugh seems to have felt that his wife would be able to figure out where he was.

The First World War saw the advent of airpower and Lord Hugh recorded this in his letters:

'An English aeroplane came down close to one of my piquets and stampeded the horses. Luckily I have got them back, they all belong to Gerry's troop.'

'Gerry' was Lieutenant Hon Gerald Ward.

Corporal of Horse Lloyd described what it was like to be a cavalryman on active service:

'The part played by an individual soldier in a big operation … is insignificant. His chief interest and responsibility throughout the whole scheme is to keep himself, his horse and his weapons in the best possible condition; to endeavour always to have a bite in his haversack, corn in his horse's nosebag, and a full complement of ammunition in his pouches … We lived a "here today and gone tomorrow" life. Billets were unthought of. We simply got out of the saddle and slept, when we had the chance, on the ground beside our horses.'

By now the Allied frontline had reached the Channel coast on the same day that the German Army took Ostend and Zeebrugge. Soon Belgian engineers, with the authority of the King of the Belgians, would blow up the sluice gates allowing the sea to inundate the low-lying areas and effectively shorten the front-line. On 16 October Lord Hugh's squadron was in action again. This time a patrol under Sir Philip Brocklehurst came under close range fire from a machine gun on the outskirts of Staden. Trooper Henley was killed outright. Lord Hugh wrote:

'Phillip Brocklehurst and patrol bumped into a concealed machine gun yesterday. It opened fire at 40 yards and only one man and one horse were killed. Cromer was with him and Phillip told me he behaved awfully well and never turned a hair and remained riding quietly behind him although some of the others went very quickly.'

Historians still debate the value, or folly, of deploying mounted soldiers in the age of barbed wire and machine guns. The machine guns used by both British and German armies were essentially the same weapons patented by the American inventor Hiram Maxim in 1885. Clearly when well sited machine guns were deployed on the battlefield, protected by barbed wire entanglements, it was nearly suicidal to use cavalry. In other phases of warfare when the armies were manoeuvring the ability to rapidly deploy soldiers on horseback still had an important role. Ironically towards the end of the war 1/LG was reformed as No 1 (Life Guards) Battalion Guards Machine-Gun Regiment.

On 15 October Lord Worsley wrote to his parents,

'It all seems so strange; if it were not for the everlasting sound of guns, which seem quite close, but are probably several miles away, one would think one was on manoeuvres. One often catches oneself wondering which day manoeuvres are going to end – and one would give a good deal to know. The day before yesterday we were in the saddle for 17 hours – scarcely off one's horse all that time – then two hours' rest and off again for 16 hours. Needless to say men and horses absolutely stone cold, but we are having an easy time now, and very nice too. We do very well in the way of food, but we've been on the move ever since we landed … Did you send out cigarettes and tobacco and pipe, or was it Alexandra? If you, thank you very much. They were very much appreciated, and as I had a pipe, I gave it to a Corporal who had broken his. Two of my drivers are just like music-hall turns and they keep us all in shrieks of laughter all the time we are halted on the road; they are priceless.'

On 16 October Sir Douglas Haig visited Sir John French who appeared to be in an overly optimistic mood and

'seemed quite satisfied with the general situation and said that the Enemy was falling back and that we would soon be in a position to round them up.'

The strategic situation was summed up by an officer from the Loyal North Lancastrian Regiment on 17 October:

'Briefly the plan of the campaign … is to advance on Roulers via Ypres, and in conjunction with the Belgian Army and the newly-formed French 10th Army, to endeavour to turn the German right wing. Our own 7th Division, originally sent out too late to relieve Antwerp, is retreating in easy stages to join the original BEF and will make us up to the grand total of seven infantry and two cavalry divisions, some 150,000 men all told; the largest number of British troops which have ever fought together in the history of England.'

The *Daily Graphic* reported:

'There is exceedingly little official news of the great battle in France and Southern Belgium, but the news is good. The Allies' forces have now reached the sea … However there is no news of the nature of the operations in this region. A Berlin despatch states that the Germans regard the present situation … with great optimism. The spirit of the German troops in France is said to be excellent. The German right wing has now received considerable reinforcement from Belgium, and it is likely that decisive fighting will begin on the Belgium frontier within a few days. The reinforced German armies will take the offensive with the greatest energy. The correspondent of the "Politiken" declares that the cry "To Calais" is echoing in the hearts of the entire German people.'

So confident were the German High Command of a comprehensive victory that they referred to the First Battle of Ypres as The Battle of Calais.

In Lord Hugh's letter on 17 October he wrote:

'I am now sitting in a farm house which we have just fortified as the Germans are all about I hope to goodness they wont (sic) attack tonight as we are very comfortable here.'

This was indicative that there was not an established frontline as it was possible for the enemy to attack the fortified farm. This must have been nerve wracking times for both sides in the conflict.

The practicalities of operational duties led to Lord Hugh wanting more supplies from home:

'Please send cigarettes and compressed tobacco if you can get some, newspapers and will you make me a khaki tunic at Sandon's. I want it made of warm stuff and not too close fitting as I want room for woollies underneath.'

Sartorial elegance had given way to pragmatism, smoking was a relief from boredom and desire for newspapers indicated the soldiers' need for information from home. The weather was a major factor and it was reported that 'the winter of 1914–15 was the worst in living memory.' Whether Lord Hugh actually got his tunic is not known for within a fortnight he was killed.

Ever cheery, Lord Hugh ended his letter: 'Love to the boys and everyone at home. We are all well and very fit. Your Hugh.'

The cavalry were used again and again to plug the gaps in the British line to prevent the German Army from breaking through. In the days before airborne reconnaissance, satellites and drones, knowing where the enemy were was somewhat hit or miss. At this stage in the war in Flanders both sides were like boxers in the dark – swinging wild haymaker punches, sometimes landing them on their opponent, often not. On 17 October the official war diary for 1/LG read:

> 'The Brigadier has much pleasure in telling the Regiments of the Brigade that before he left Zonnebeke to-day, General Lawford, Commanding the 22nd Brigade, asked him to express to the Regiments of this Brigade his thanks for the assistance they gave him and his admiration for the way they behaved in saving what might have been a critical situation.'

The 22nd Brigade commanded by Brigadier S. T. B. Lawford was part of the 7th Division and consisted of four infantry battalions including the 1st Battalion of the Royal Welch Fusiliers (1/RWF). Lord Hugh would defend Zandvoorde ridge with 1/RWF. It was apparent that the 7th Cavalry Brigade was operating shoulder to shoulder with their infantry counterparts.

On 18 October I Corps had begun to move off from their positions on the Aisne and would start arriving in the Ypres area in a few days. Lieutenant General Sir Henry Rawlinson GOC of IV Corps received orders to advance towards Menin. Unbeknown to the British the German forces had prepared themselves for their attack behind their cavalry:

> 'The screening of the advancing Fourth Army was a brilliant success. At midday on the 18th Field Marshal French was still in ignorance of our new army.'

The 7th Cavalry Brigade had again been called upon to support their infantry comrades on 19 October:

'Brigade marched to 11th kilometre stone on Roulers-Menin road. On arrival there it became heavily engaged with hostile infantry and artillery. Maintained position for 3 hours and then retired on Moorslede. Heavy casualties in 2nd LG. Regiment lost Lt Sir P Brocklehurst wounded and one man killed and 4 wounded.'

The infantry which the cavalry encountered on the road to Menin were the spearhead of the German Army. In fact it was the XXVII Reserve Corps which reported that they

'had come into contact with the 3rd British Cavalry Division which had tried to hold up the Corps … after a lively encounter the British cavalry were thrown back.'

British pilots had spotted columns of thousands of German soldiers marching fast and heading towards Ypres. One pilot reported seeing: 'Columns of Huns coming along the road from Courtrai – country black with the sods.' This was the first day of the First Battle of Ypres.

To an observer it would be patently obvious that the Allied forces were facing a significant German force of massed infantry, not merely cavalry patrols; however (according to Sir Douglas Haig's diary) this news had yet to reach the ears of Sir John French:

'Sir John stated that he estimated the enemy's strength on the front Ostend to Menin, at about one corps, not more.'

He then proceeded to give Haig orders to advance with French and British cavalry covering his flanks. The 7th Division abandoned their planned advance towards Menin and withdrew to their original positions.

Chapter 9

The First Battle of Ypres

To call the land to the east of Ypres uninteresting is being rather kind. It was described as

> 'open country; just a few villages broke up the solitude of the dreary plain – a flat area of cultivated fields bordered by rows of poplar and willow trees.'

The area consists of low lying farmland drained by streams and ditches called 'beeks'. The word Flanders means flooded plain and the water table is so high that digging deep trenches is virtually impossible.

According to historian C. R. M. F. Cruttwell the ground was: 'Flat, naked and oozy country.' Flanders also features several low ridges such as Pilkem, Passchendaele, Messines, Gheluveld and Zandvoorde. The tactical importance of these ridges, some only 200 foot higher than the surrounding plain, could not be overestimated. Once in the hands of the enemy artillery observation officers the surrounding area became untenable to the opposition as any movement would bring down a barrage of shells.

The First Battle of Ypres could be described by a military historian as an 'encounter battle' where units are committed to the action in a piecemeal fashion to shore up the frontline. To a lay person the battle was a 'scrap' where the Germans were attempting to force their 4th Army through a huge set of doors, as their 6th Army stood guard. Every time they appeared to be succeeding the allies managed somehow to hold them back by 'putting up' their line. 'Putting up' was achieved by ignoring the normally strict adherence to division, brigade or battalion formations; anybody capable of firing a rifle was pushed up into the front line. The British were outnumbered by odds of at least 5 to 1 and consistently requested, and received, support from their French allies. The continuous fighting ebbed and flowed; dying down in one sector only to commence elsewhere and much of it was hand to hand. There was no time to construct deep connecting trenches (indeed there were few spades and even less barbed wire); a scraping in the soil or loop holing a wall or building would prove to be invaluable.

First Ypres was defined by Robin Neillands as a 'soldiers' battle'; holding ground and killing Germans outweighed any opportunity for strategic planning for high command. Survival was all that mattered! The First Battle of Ypres changed military doctrine. In 1861 in the United States General 'Stonewall' Jackson told junior officers: 'When war does come, my advice is to draw the sword and throw away the scabbard.' He probably meant that surrender was not an option. It could be that he thought that battle changes things fundamentally. The thought of sheathing your sword after the war

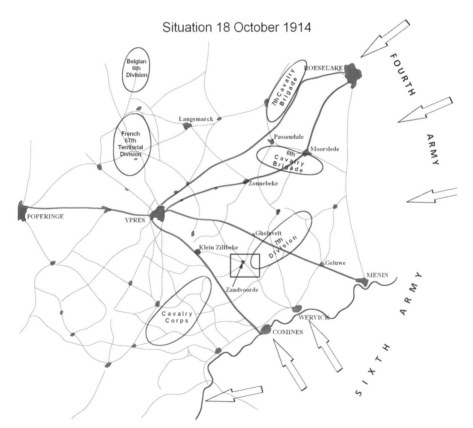

Map 3: Official History map showing position on 18 October. (*David Parkland*)

would not have been feasible as this represented returning to the pre-war status quo. The First World War changed everything.

First Ypres lasted four weeks from 19 October to 20/22 November and saw some of the most desperate fighting of the war. It is surprising that the thinly stretched Allied forces clung on at all let alone brought the juggernaut of the German Army to a dead stop. The battle was described by Sir Harold Wernher (a comrade of Bendor, the Duke of Westminster):

> 'The situation was extremely confused. We'd get the order to advance a mile or two, and then we'd get the order to fall back a mile or two. Every town and village would change hands several times in the course of perhaps a single week. No-one below the rank of General knew who was supposed to be where – not we, not the Hun. No-one. We all simply moved back and forth, waiting for some sort of order to clamp down on the situation – and, of course, fighting like mad all the time. That is, when we could get at the enemy. Often we lost sight of him altogether.'

The scene was set by Colonel Ralph Bingham:

> 'The situation became grimmer and grimmer until at last the final furious battle for Ypres developed. The enemy on our front had been actively reconnoitering our position for days. They had, of course, discovered that the line was held merely by handfuls of dismounted cavalry and that there were practically no reserves. There were, in fact, none. Actually four miles of front were being held by 600 dismounted cavalry with nothing behind them. It was a good bluff!'

In many respects the bluff was accepted by the Germans. The British General Staff reports on a German officer being captured during the battle and whilst being led away asked his escort 'Now I am out of it, do tell me where your reserves are concealed; in what woods are they?' When told that there were no reserves the German was incredulous and refused to believe it.

Lieut. Ralph Bingham.
Ist Life Guards.

Lieutenant (later Colonel) Ralph Bingham 1/LG at Windmill Hill Camp in 1914. (*Christina Broom*)

'Apparently it was inconceivable to the German General Staff that we should stand to fight unless we had superior numbers; and these not being visible in the field, they must be hidden away somewhere.'

The Germans also concluded that the paltry British front line was merely an outpost line positioned in front of the main defences; in fact that was the main defence. By the end of the battle,

'many of the [British] Regiments … were technically "annihilated". Their officers went; their senior NCOs went; they were worn out to the last stage of mental and physical exhaustion by sleeplessness, and by unceasing digging and fighting. And still they held on … with stubborn determination which nothing could break through; and to the Battalions on whose soldiers fell the main weight of this burden is due the homage of all who stayed at home.'

On 19 October Lord Worsley's machine-gun section was in action at Roulers covering the withdrawal of the French 5th Cavalry Division in the face of an enemy infantry attack. Captain Foster, adjutant of RHG, recorded in his diary,

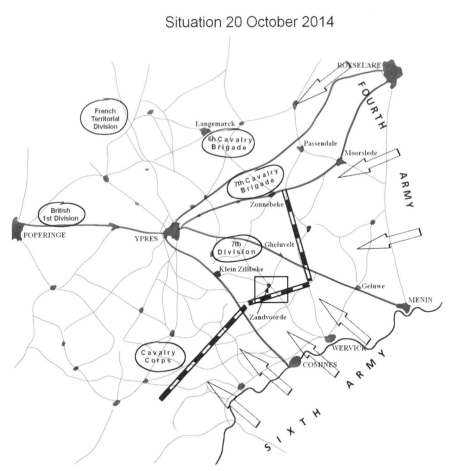

Situation 20 October 2014

Map 4: Official History map showing positions on 20 October. The section of the line held by the 3rd Cavalry Division was being attacked by German Cavalry units. (*David Parkland*)

'The appearance of the German infantry appears to have been unexpected, it was thought the fighting would be against Cavalry only, instead of which the Germans brought up an Army Corps, and there were only two Cavalry regiments to oppose them.'

Seeing the civilian population of Roulers flee their burning town Lord Worsley wrote,

'The most dreadful part of the war is the poor refugees: One's heart bleeds for them ... leaving every mortal thing and rushing off ... We very often billet in empty houses and find meals left on the table all ready, and the cows all longing to be milked, poor things.'

On 20 October the battle raged ferociously. The British artillery took a massive toll on the opposition. A gunner supporting the 7th Division reported: 'Our battery fires all day. The news is that we are slaughtering them, as they are attacking in mass formation.' No longer were the British fighting off enemy cavalry units but were bearing the brunt of massed German infantry. At Le Pilly the 2nd Battalion Royal Irish Regiment was attacked by German artillery and infantry all day long:

'At 3 pm Major Daniell ordered the survivors to fix bayonets and the few whole men were joined by as many of the wounded as could walk and hold a weapon. In this counter attack Daniell was killed and his battalion destroyed.'

Such was the intensity of the fighting that the battalion lost 257 killed, 290 captured (almost all were wounded) and only about 30 made it back to their own lines.

The 1/LG war diary records:

'At 10 am orders were received to hold on to this line as long as possible as 1st Corps was expected at 1 pm. A Battalion of French 79th Territorial Regiment which retired through the position was intercepted and asked to support the Regiment, this they did. The enemy did not advance nearer than 1,500 yards from the position, but at 12.30 pm the town of Passchendeale which had been held by a French Cavalry Division, fell into the hands of the enemy and the Regiment was forced to retire on St Julien, where the Brigade had been ordered to concentrate on retirement.'

The taciturn war diary entry does not convey the human tragedies on the battlefield. One of the host of fatalities that day was from the Cavendish family and a close friend of Lord Hugh. Son of the 8th Duke of Devonshire and raised at Chatsworth in Derbyshire, Major Lord John Spencer Cavendish DSO, of 1/LG, was killed in action on 20 October. Henry 'Harry' Lascelles wrote to Lady Edward Cavendish, John's mother, five days after the action breaking the terrible news:

October 25 1914 My dear Aunt Emma

I can't tell you with what sorrow I write you this letter to tell you how poor dear John was killed. We were holding rather an awkward position & were being heavily attacked by German infantry. John with his Squadron was on our left flank, & when walking forward to his advanced troop, came under the fire of a Maxim gun, & was shot dead on the spot. I was speaking to him not 10 minutes before. We had to retire subsequently & leave the body where it lay, but arrangements have been made to have it buried by the farmer & the spot marked; being between our lines it has been impossible to get at it at present. Edward Wyndham is sending you home his uniform, glasses and sword, at the earliest opportunity, the rest of his things are being distributed among his men. There are also some 400 francs in cash. I can[']t tell you dear Aunt Emma what a loss he will be to us, he was always so steady and dependable and everyone was devoted to him, but you will always have the satisfaction of knowing, that he died a death worthy of the name Cavendish. Both our Colonels have been wounded, so I am now in command of the Regiment. Goodbye dear Aunt Emma with much love.

From your affect[ionate] nephew

Harry'

On this day the Germans had taken the strategically important village of Passchendaele. The war diary of 2/LG for 20 October reads:

'Marched at 5am to untrench near Westroosebeke. On arrival at our line found French infantry partially untrenched already, but they promptly withdrew, so we defended the Westroosebeke-Paschendaele road by trench to W of it in the order from the right 1st Life Guards, R H Gds, ourselves, Royal Dragoons, 10th Hussars, French troops on the left. My horses were concealed behind a wood but soon they had to be moved further back to avoid shells. This led to some confusion as the Squadrons did not know where their horses had gone. This was the first attempt of the Household Cavalry to dig trenches, and they were very welcome as the shell fire for about 2 hours was severe. German attempts to cross the main road with infantry were easily checked by our rifle fire, but the French on the extreme left retired without any warning to us of their intention. The VI Cavalry Brigade consequently had to go, and we on our turn had to go too in successive Regiments from the left, my Squadrons holding farms to cover the retirement. We were lucky to disengage without losses, as we had to go a long way on foot, and the led horses were in some confusion as stated above.'

Sir Douglas Haig was General Officer Commanding I Corps and, despite Sir John French's order to advance on 19 October, he moved his forces into Flanders and on 21 October ordered them into defensive positions around Ypres. Haig described the chaotic situation:

'All roads crowded with French Territorial troops … advance of 1st Division delayed … The attack of the 2nd Division was consequently delayed … Fighting was hard and came to bayonet work … without warning the French Cavalry guarding our left flank is ordered to retire west of the Canal!'

If Ypres could be envisaged topographically as being in the centre of a saucer, Haig positioned his forces around the saucer's rim along the low ridges of Pilkem, Messines and eventually Zandvoorde. It must be pointed out that the vital ground was in fact along the Menin Road, especially the villages of Gheluvelt, Passendeale and Hooge. Loss of these vantage points was thought to compromise Ypres and, if the Germans could force their way through, they would be within a few miles of the town itself.

During this critical period for the Household Cavalry at Zandvoorde Haig was based at the White Chateau a few miles behind the front line along the vital Ypres to Menin road. Whether the desperate fighting for Gheluvelt directly to Haig's front was given a higher priority than the defence of Zandvoorde ridge is speculation. It is true that Haig was personally involved in the fighting to stem the withdrawal from Gheluvelt becoming a headlong rout back into Ypres. There are accounts of him advancing on horseback on 31 October to witness the situation first hand and to steady his troops.

The British high command took the decision to go on the defensive by ordering that

'action against enemy will be continued tomorrow on general line now held, which will be strongly entrenched.'

Quartermasters from the 7th Division desperately scoured Ypres for entrenching materiel – they found only 20 spades and no barbed wire.

Although still optimistic French had to concede that he was faced with: 'Several *Landwehr* or similar divisions – nothing of any quantity or consequence.' In fact he had massively underestimated his opposition and was facing substantial elements of the Fourth and Sixth Armies. On the following day, during a meeting with General Joffre, French requested 'facilities to make a great entrenched camp at Boulogne to take the whole Expeditionary Force.' The British commander must have finally appreciated the dire straits he was in and wanted to establish a bastion by the coast. General Joffre refused the request.

The lack of preparedness for trench warfare in this phase of the war is clear from the following quote:

'We are ordered to take up a defensive position, and commence to dig ourselves in. I go to a nearby farm with some men and commandeer all the spades I can find, and also remove sundry doors, which will come in useful for overhead cover.'

Throughout 20 October the 7th Division were subjected to intense infantry and artillery attacks, but the line was held. Back in England, however, the public would have had little idea of the detail of the fighting:

'Official news of the vastly important operations in Northern France and West Flanders is still very scant. It is evident, however, from the brief official communiqués issued in Paris that the fighting in both areas is fierce and desperate. The news is good.'

The phrase 'the news is good' is repeated by Lord Hugh in his letter on 27 October almost like a mantra. The effect on morale of a positive message from the leader cannot be undervalued. Lord Hugh's letters home were always upbeat, although one knows from contemporary accounts (such as from Crofton and Lloyd) that he must have been enduring terrible conditions. This is the epitome of stoicism. General Sir Anthony Farrar-Hockley stated that 'the corps staff had drawn a line on the map for 7th Division to hold without regard to contours, and unhappily General Capper the divisional commander had to accept it.' His infantry were therefore dug in on forward slopes. With his predilection for offensive action Tommy Capper would have found forward slope positions a natural jumping-off point.

On 21 October the southernmost part of the 7th Division trench line ended at Zandvoorde. 'The news is good,' was also a common theme early in the battle in Sir John French's telegraphs to Lord Kitchener, Secretary of State for War. On the night of 21 October Sir John wrote: 'In my opinion the enemy are vigorously playing their last card and I am confident they will fail.' Even on 25 October French 'reported that the situation was growing more favourable hour by hour … my anxiety is over.' It seems obvious in retrospect that he did not have a complete grasp of the strength of the enemy forces ranged against him.

The 3rd Cavalry Division was released from its holding position at Zonnebeke and was detailed with spanning the ground from Zandvoorde to the Cavalry Corps at Hollebeke, Wytschate and Messines. At this time the

British were tenuously holding a line about 16 miles long from Bixschoote to Hollebeke via Becleaere whilst waiting anxiously for the arrival of more infantry battalions from the south before the increasing German assaults overwhelmed them:

'The line of defence was ridiculously extended – extended indeed far beyond the recognized limits of effective resistance, and there was no reserve available with which to strengthen any threatened spot.'

On 22 October Lord Hugh wrote home:

'My Own Darling, We have had a real doing for the last 3 days and now we are waiting saddled up in reserve, a devil of a battle going on in front and a few stray shells coming our way. We have been fighting hard for the last few days. Phillip Brocklehurst was shot through the shoulder three days ago he is hit bad, try and see him if he goes home. He is a great loss. Dolly has gone to the base and I suppose home with his old complaint. I have just heard that poor old John Cavendish has been killed. I am so sorry for Aunt Emma. This is a rotten letter but it is being written under difficulties. The Second have been awfully unlucky and have lost about 6 officers killed and wounded. We were all complimented on the way we helped the infantry yesterday. I didn't think we had done much but we helped to fill in a gap. Another of my Corporals is wounded Cram. Not badly. I am awfully well very short of sleep. Bless you Your Hugh.'

'Dolly' was the nickname of His Highness Adolphus the Duke of Teck.
    The Second' were the 2nd Regiment of Life Guards.
    A few days later Philip Brocklehurst was recovering at home in Macclesfield where he wrote to Lady Hugh Grosvenor in glowing terms about Lord Hugh:

'He was very well and doing splendidly, as of course he would, and I cannot tell you how sorry I was to leave him. He was a splendid squadron leader and his leadership always gave me the utmost confidence which is the most I can say of a man. I am not used to being led and have always done my work my own way, therefore the man whose leadership appeals to me must be the very best. I am so stupid to get hit so early in the campaign when I know your husband wants everyman in the squadron, but I hope I shall be able to get back to him before very long.'

In typical understatement Lord Hugh refers to a *'real doing for the last 3 days'*. The battle was described by David Lomas as:

'In the centre, successive waves of the 54th [German] Reserve Division and the 3rd Cavalry Division pressed hard against the 2nd Green Howards and 2nd Royal Scots Fusiliers, part of the 21st Brigade. The battalion wavered briefly and some German troops broke through between two units. They ran into another company of Royal Scots at Polderhoek Chateau who sent them reeling back with sustained fire. The line reformed and the Germans withdrew, leaving behind a terrible legacy of dead and wounded.'

A first-hand account of the situation was:

'The battle rages on all sides and the noise of bursting shells and the spluttering of rifle and machine-gun fire is deafening. From the meagre news that filters down to us, we gather there are literally hordes of Germans in front of us, and not only has our own advance been brought to a standstill, but on portions of the battle front we are hard put to hold our own. From the captured documents we understand it is the intention of the Germans to drive us away from the Channel ports of Calais and Boulogne, and events in the near future may become critical.'

A gap had opened in the British line and Rawlinson ordered the 7th Cavalry Brigade to mount up and act as a mobile reserve in case the Germans discovered the break in the line and tried to pour through. The 7th Cavalry Brigade made up of 1/LG, 2/LG and RHG were led by Brigadier General

Charles Toller McMorrough Kavanagh. His brigade gained the soubriquet 'Kavanagh's Fire Brigade' by plugging gaps in the line during the First Battle of Ypres. What this actually meant was:

> 'The brigade not in the line stood saddled up a short distance behind in reserve. Wherever any part of the line within a few miles was hard pressed or in danger of being broken, the reserve brigade was called upon. It straight away galloped to the danger point, dismounted, and going in with the bayonet, put things in order again. It then held the line till relieved, after which it got back to its position in reserve. Our horses ceased to be employed as cavalry horses. Their role was similar to that played later by the omnibus, the rapid conveyance of rifle-and-bayonet soldiers to the line. The exciting scampering along country roads and through neat villages gave place to an existence comparable only to that of a water-rat in a swamp. We soon ceased to worry about roads, and always travelled across country, wading to our destination on a bee-line through the mud.'

Going into action in this manner meant leaving the riderless horses with the No 3 (often a saddler/farrier or member of the regimental staff) who were responsible for five or six mounts. This left each squadron with perhaps 80 effective soldiers to enter the fray.

Chapter 10

Zandvoorde

On 22/23 October the 3rd Cavalry Division started their nine days in possession of the Zandvoorde trenches:

> 'They formed the most dangerous position in the whole line of defence, being in the form of a promontory which jutted out defiantly into the enemy's country … Their chief attraction, from the purely military point of view, lay in the fact that they were on the crest of a ridge some 120 feet high. Their weakness lay in the fact that they were practically surrounded by the enemy.'

Haig is reported as saying: 'If we give way the war's lost. Positions will be held to the last man and the last round.'

10th Hussars (6th Cavalry Brigade) relieved the 2nd Battalion Scots Guards (10th Brigade) from the Zandvoorde trenches. The Scots Guards

The Scots Guards manning the Zandvoorde trenches before they were handed over to 3rd Cavalry Division. (*Imperial War Museum*)

were to take over the trenches at nearby Kruiseik. The idea was that the 6th and 7th Cavalry brigades were take turns to man the trenches: 'A portion of the line was allotted to the Division, and, when possible, the two Brigades relieved each other every forty-eight hours.'

The very act simply of getting into the Zandvoorde trenches was far from simple as Corporal of Horse Lloyd described, after a long journey on foot at night through the ruins of Zandvoorde village under sporadic enemy machine-gun fire:

> 'We then set off crawling up into the necks of our long cavalry cloaks which got under our knees. As luck would have it, we actually crawled in the darkness right between two of our own trenches, thus getting in front of a position held by Sergeant Dapper Smith and a few men. Dapper was a blood-thirsty fellow, so he turned the fire of his section on us at point-blank range. By a miracle none of us was hit, and when the language issuing from the trench caused the true state of affairs to dawn upon us. Tom Birch called them a few complimentary names and requested them, none too politely, to turn it off. They ceased fire and we set about distributing ourselves in the line.'

Unfortunately the trenches … 'a series of holes, for all the world like large graves,' were full to capacity with men. Lloyd almost bribed his way into an already packed trench with a quantity of cigarettes. One soldier, Harry Pudney, had tried in vain to get into a trench:

> 'The poor devil was about done up and babbling with indignation. For half an hour he had been crawling about in a spray of bullets, seeking an opportunity to hold a position of the line for his King and country and being grossly insulted everywhere he showed his nose.'

During the night

> 'one man at a time stood up and kept a lookout. The others squatted huddled up in the bottom of the trench and slept with one eye open. When the night was well advanced, the senior sergeant, Snuffy Webb,

Major (later Lieutenant Colonel) Edgar Brassey was wounded by artillery fire and patched up by Lord Hugh. (*Christina Broom*)

crawled along the back of the holes and gave each of us a tot of rum. It went down to our very toes and made us as warm as toast, but without food and drink as we were it created an intense thirst afterwards.'

That night the Gordon Highlanders manning the trenches to the left of the Life Guards opened fire on the Germans. Captain Stanley, anticipating an assault, passed a request from trench to trench to ask what the Gordon Highlanders planned to do if an attack came – the reply passed back from trench to trench caused a cheer to go up among the Life Guards: 'The Gordons will hold on to the last man!'

The war diary of 1/Life Guards records on 23 October:

'Klein Zillebeke Oct 23, 08.30 am – Brigade ordered to relieve 6th Cavalry Brigade in trenches on line Zandvoorde-Hollebeke Road. On arrival below position Brigade Staff rode forward with Commanding Officers and Squadron Leaders to have position of trenches pointed out to them by 6th Brigade. While standing on crest of position two shells burst over them and all were hit except three Squadron leaders of Regiment. Officers of Brigade Staff only had their clothing torn, but Major Brassey had his ear grazed and Lieutenant Marquess of Tweeddale had his lips cut by shrapnel bullet. It was then decided that it was not safe to relieve the trenches before dark, so Brigade returned to Klein Zillebeke till dusk, when it again advanced and took over trenches.'

Lord Hugh described this incident in one of his letters:

'Some of us had a lucky escape a few days ago. We were going to relieve the 10th in the trenches and had walked up to see the way they were placed. General Kavanagh Col Fergusson. Edgar. Algy. Hardy and myself and one or two more. We were foolishly standing in a little heap when 2 shells burst almost at our feet. Kavanagh got a bullet through his foot without touching him. Col Fergusson got some into his leg and was wounded luckily he is fat and was just in front of me. Edgar had a little chip taken out of his ear which I bandaged with great skill.

Jazekan had both lips split but not bad, everybody else had holes in their clothes except Algy, Leonard and I. It was funny to see everyone duck and I laughed I must say.'

'The 10th' were the 10th (Prince of Wales's Own) Royal Hussars which formed part of the 6th Cavalry Brigade; 'General Kavanagh' was Brigadier-General C. M. Kavanagh Commanding the 7th Cavalry Brigade; 'Edgar' was Major, later Lieutenant Colonel, E. H. Brassey and 'Jazakan' was Captain the Marquis of Tweeddale. It seems that Lord Hugh found humour an effective coping mechanism when faced with stressful situations.

Not far away on that day thousands of poorly trained German volunteers attacked *en masse* at Langemarck. Some were reported to be advancing arm-in-arm, singing and wearing their university caps. The British gunners, firing Shrapnel rounds at close range, took a terrible toll.

This is the view from the Zandvoorde to Hollebeke Road near to where Lord Hugh and his fellow officers came artillery under fire. (*M. J. McBride*)

The experiences of Langemarck, and later at Zandvoorde, caused the Germans to change their tactics. They were not to make daylight massed infantry assaults again.

Accounts from the 1st Battalion Gloucester Regiment give an impression of the conditions in a defensive position:

'The enemy … then began to push their attack … The wounded who could by any means work a rifle were brought into action again. Private King who was shot through the left shoulder propped himself up in a corner of the traverse and worked his rifle with one hand. The gallantry of Private Cratchley is worthy of record. At this time he was hit in the left jaw by a bullet which passed out of the right side of the neck. Blood was pouring from the wound and he fell to the floor of the trench. The wounded in the trench put a field dressing on his wound as best they could. He then crawled to the corner of the traverse, got to his feet and continued firing at the enemy.'

Also on 23 October the 2nd Battalion the Wiltshire Regiment from the 21st Brigade were overwhelmed at Reutel from all sides by three battalions of the German 224th Reserve Regiment leaving the road to Ypres wide open. In desperation, Major General Capper assembled a force of Northumberland Hussars and assorted support troops (clerks, orderlies and cooks) to block the German advance. One of the cooks was apparently only armed with a soup ladle! Realising the dire straits of the 7th Division Haig sent the 5th Brigade under Brigadier R. C. B. Haking with his four infantry battalions to assist. On 24 October the Household Cavalry had occupied the Zandvoorde trenches. According to the official war diary:

'Remained in trenches for 48 hours. Trenches heavily shelled all day. Both nights heavy firing opened about 9 pm, but no actual attack was made. Firing lasted about ½ an hour and the same was repeated at about 2am.'

Although Lord Hugh's C Squadron was meant to be relieved from their duties in the trenches on 25 October they had to remain for a further 24 hours because '6th Bde had only 2 Regiments with which to relieve 3.' Essentially one squadron was being asked to cover for a whole regiment. This was stretching the 'thin red line' ludicrously thin.

It is worth recounting first-hand what it was like for cavalrymen to occupy trenches at this point in the war:

'We now dismount to continue the march on foot, and hand over the horses to one of our No. 3s (horse-holders) ... I remove my spurs and prepare for a muddy wet filthy walk. It is now dark as pitch and we stumble along a lane until we reach a partially destroyed village called Zillebeke. Not a light nor a living soul appears. Silhouettes of ruined houses mark our dismal journey through the rain and mist.

'On entering the village we suddenly come under machine-gun fire and a stream of bullets whiz over us. We rush to the battered wall to take cover for a short time while it lasts, and we proceed crouching along the ruins until it ceases ... We stumble on, my machine gunners alongside me carrying the guns and tripods on their shoulders, with others behind with the belts and ammunition boxes. A terrific musketry fire is going on all round, and every now and then the big guns join in, so the noise is considerable. After about 10 minutes it dies away as suddenly as it began. When the musketry has more or less ceased we move on.

'We climb a bank and over into a muddy field, down a slope we go, the mud over our ankles, over a small stream, then up a slope, at the top of which 200 yards away is our line of trenches which we are to occupy just below the crest ... There has been a considerable fight during the afternoon and we have to wait at the sloppy muddy mouth of the entrance to the trench while the casualties are being removed ... After a long wait, half frozen in the mud, we filed down the narrow trench which led to our front line ... We stumbled down the trench making slow progress, as it was very narrow and half way up was blocked by a dead man, over whom we slipped and fell in the darkness ... A man lay across the front trench very badly wounded, I think in the lungs, for he moaned a lot, and as he breathed he hissed like a punctured tyre. He was removed after a great deal of difficulty and delay.

The night was bitterly cold, but very clear, and the stars shone like electric lamps. We settled down for a most uncomfortable night, huddling together in heaps, and eat cold bully beef and chocolate. About 20 yards out beyond our trenches we heard wounded Germans, the result of ineffective attacks in the afternoon, calling out in a plaintive and mournful manner. They were like Banshees. Then one by one the cries ceased presumably as the men died. We slept for intervals of half an hour or so during the night.'

It is easy to imagine that Lord Hugh endured similar trench experiences. As he spared his wife the horrors of trench warfare we must rely on the testimony of fellow officers, such as Morgan Crofton, to provide an unexpurgated account. If getting into a trench was difficult, getting out could also be a challenge as Corporal of Horse Lloyd recounted:

'Filing out was going to be no simple matter. The business of getting out of a hole six feet deep, with its sides covered with a foot of sticky mud, while the rain fell in sheets, would have presented a sea-lion with serious difficulties.'

If Lord Hugh and his cavalrymen were enduring the awfulness of primitive trench warfare an infantry battalion to their front was in an even more perilous position. The Household Cavalry were forced into an extraordinary mission to ease the suffering and help this stricken battalion try and extricate themselves from the pulverising they were getting. Since 22 October the 2nd Battalion the Border Regiment had been holding on to an exposed position between the Zandvoorde road and the Kruiseik-Wervik road. They were shelled heavily and remorselessly by German artillery without response from the British guns:

'Their relaxation during those six days consisted of counting the shells directed at them, and speculating as to the accuracy of the next shot.'

The battalion suffered over one hundred casualties a day. In an attempt to relieve the pressure from the Border Regiment the Household Cavalry were pushed forwards:

'Gordon Wilson's Royal Horse Guards which were at Klein Zillebeke were ordered to make a "mounted demonstration" towards Kruiseke in effect a show of force to distract attention away from the embattled Border Regiment. A squadron of 1/Life Guards under Captain Hugh Grosvenor had been in the Kruiseke trenches with the Border Regiment since the previous day and were no doubt as surprised as the Germans were by the arrival of the Blues just as it was getting dusk. According to a Blues officer, "We rode onto the crest between the two trenches held by Hugh Grosvenor's squadron, and here the Germans spotted us and we came in for a hail of Shrapnel and bullets. My horse was hit in the shoulder and I got into a trench in which were Hugh Grosvenor and Gerry Ward. They seemed surprised at our selecting this spot for a point-to-point. Grosvenor's squadron came in after 72 hours in the trenches."'

This mission was described by Corporal of Horse Lloyd:

'The Brigade rode at once to the danger zone and dismounted for action. The Blues were detailed to lead the attack; we went over as second wave, and the 2nd Life Guards were in reserve. The Blues went through the original German line, which they occupied. We followed some two hundred yards behind and when the Blues had cleared the old enemy line we dug in where we stood. The Blues then withdrew through us and we handed over our hastily-dug line to the infantry two hours late. We then returned to our horses and got back to Klein Zillebeke. The Germans thought the whole Cavalry Corps was behind us, ready to gallop their trenches, and turned every available gun on the valley behind us. This is exactly what we wanted, as it relieved the pressure on the Twentieth Brigade.'

Captain the Lord Alastair Innes-Ker of The Blues was awarded the Distinguished Service Order for showing conspicuous courage when the Blues, by bold and rapid movement across the front of two German Cavalry Regiments, were able to extricate the 20th Infantry Brigade from Kruiseecke.'

Eventually the 300 remaining soldiers of the Border Regiment withdrew from their position on 27 October. Captain Charles Cholmondeley of the Border Regiment died in this action. He was the youngest son of the 2nd son of the 3rd Marquess Charles Cholmondeley and born 1880; he joined the Militia in 1900 and after four months joined the 2nd Border Regiment becoming a Captain 1910. He was another casualty from the Cheshire landed gentry and would have been well known to Lord Hugh. With the retirement from the position held by the Border Regiment one less obstacle remained for the Germans attacking the Zandvoorde trenches held by the Household Cavalry. The scene was now set for the final attack.

The weather became worse with heavy rain and a drop in temperature. On 26 October Lord Hugh got a message through to 1/Life Guards:

'Private Whitehead was killed last night. There appears to be a considerable force of the enemy to my front and to my right front. They approach to within about seven hundred yards at night. Our shells have not been near them on this flank. Are we to be relieved to-night, should like some rations. The man I sent, Private Price, with message to you yesterday has not returned.'

5298 Private George Edward Whitehead of 6th Dragoons (Inniskilling) died on 25 October.

At 22.00 hours C Squadron returned to their billets having endured 72 hours in muddy holes in the ground under enemy artillery fire. The report stated that 'they had been through a rough spell. Their chief troubles had been cold, wet clothes and hunger.'

It is reasonable to deduce that elements of the German 39th Division were probing the British trench line trying to find their location and strength. Lord Hugh's comments on the ineffectiveness of the British artillery would become all too apparent on 30 October when the main attack was launched.

This is Kruiseke Straat today with the Zantvoorde (*sic*) British Cemetery on the left. The Kruiseke Trenches would possibly have followed the line of the road with the fire trench facing towards the right. (*M. J. McBride*)

Generally a shortage of artillery ammunition was compounded by many of the guns wearing out due to intensity of use.

The *Daily Graphic* was aware that a decisive battle was brewing:

'The destiny of Europe and the whole world continues to be at stake in the Flemish plains and to the shores of the sea. Germany is fighting desperately, and hopes to be able to dominate the cliffs of Dover from Calais. Nevertheless that which the Emperor has at stake … is his crown, the unity of his country, his fortune and his life.'

If the British papers were in the dark about the situation, Lord Tweedmouth of the Royal Horse Guards was only too painfully aware:

'There are some remarkably good shots in front of our trenches and snipers in concealed positions who pick you off for a certainty if you show your head above your trench. The siting of these trenches are a perfect example of what trenches should not be, being on a forward slope and in full view of the enemy's trenches and observation posts. Once occupied it is impossible to reinforce them in daylight or to take ammunition up or to communicate between the trenches. I believe General Kavanagh wanted to evacuate them and occupy the reverse slope but was not allowed to.'

The questionable tactic of the forward slope positioning of trenches was recorded in Sir Douglas Haig's diary at this time:

'It was sad to see fine troops like the 7th Division reduced to inefficiency through ignorance of their leaders in having placed them in trenches on the forward slopes where enemy could see and so effectively shell them.'

On the following day Lord Hugh wrote his penultimate letter home:

'My Darling, I am afraid I haven't written for some time but ever since the 19th with the exception of one day we have been hard at it fighting most of the time.

'On the 21st we were hurried up to the infantry line to support an infantry brigade who had been having a bad time, we did not do much but we were thanked profusely by the infantry general. On the 22nd we had more or less a day off. On the 23rd we went into trenches my Squadron was there without being relieved for 3 days and nights under shell fire most of the time and the Germans made feeble night attacks each night so sleep was impossible. One night was horribly wet. We were lucky again lost 2 men killed and 2 wounded. We have had one night off and most of today but we go back again this afternoon but the battle is progressing formally so I expect we should have an easy time. Poor Levinge was killed the day before yesterday. I am sick of behaving like a foot soldier manning trenches and running about turnip fields and I expect we shall get a move on soon. Our transport for the brigade was heavily shelled the day before yesterday 40 horses killed. Jane escaped. No men hurt.'

The loss of the horses Lord Hugh referred to due to an enemy artillery barrage was recorded by Corporal of Horse Lloyd:

'The Germans began trying to fill their field with 'Jack Johnsons' (high explosive shells). The field was some two hundred yards square, yet from a distance of at least ten miles the enemy landed a large howitzer shell right in the middle of it every two minutes. Some twenty 'coal boxes' (shells) arrived in all. The men lay flat on the ground and nobody was hit; but the unfortunate horses, standing up and tied to lines, got the full benefit of it.'

Lord Hugh would have been distressed by the death of so many horses as well as his comrades such as Sir Richard Levigne who was shot and immediately buried; the following day it emerged that he still had the squadron's pay in the inside pocket of his jacket. He was duly disinterred and the money recovered.

The death of Sir Richard Levinge was also described by Corporal of Horse Lloyd:

'It seemed as if everybody had become bored to the limit with cold and waiting and was resolved to smarten things up somehow or other. In the trench to our right a man was killed by a bullet through his head, and his companions, instead of growing more cautious, kept on firing at nothing, exposing themselves, and wasting ammunition. They paid dearly for their rashness, for before morning broke they had Sir Richard Levinge and three others killed in the same way.'

After three days and nights in the trenches near Zandvoorde Lord Hugh was obviously hoping for a rest for his battle weary troops. Unfortunately this was not to be. The use of cavalrymen in the trenches was deplored by Lord Hugh and his fellow officers.

As Morgan Crofton put it, 'It takes two years to make a cavalryman. If the cavalry are to be used as infantry, or in trench work, it is being uselessly frittered away and as it is the most expensive arm, it is useless extravagance to waste it.' He also referred to trench warfare as 'this damned mudlarking,' and that 'trenches ruin the cavalry spirit' – sentiments probably shared by all cavalry officers. Even the very ground of Flanders seemed to conspire against the soldiers. The mud of Flanders impeded movement significantly: 'The soil stuck to our boots in an awful way. Each foot had a lump on it as big as a football and weighing 20lb.'

In his letters Lord Hugh did not convey the sickening terror he would have felt being shelled by artillery. Morgan Crofton describes the experience:

'About 10 o'clock the first shells fell over our trench. These increased in number very shortly until about 10.30 when a perfect inferno was raging over the whole of our line of the trench. It was all very shaky. We lay prone on the bottom of the trench, but from time to time looked out … to see if there were any signs of a German attack. The shells pitched very close in front, the Germans obviously had the correct range, and tore the parapet, thus causing the sandy sides of the trench to silt it. We were half stunned, choked with sand and half-buried in the debris. The explosions deafened us … Wounded men with panic stricken faces now began to drag themselves painfully along the crowded and narrow way. Some were hit in the head, some in the stomach and one or two in the leg, all by (shell) splinters.'

Lloyd also recounted the effect of being shelled:

'A few times that day we sat down tight in the bottom of the trench and waited with baited breath while the enemy sent salvoes of shells … when a shell dropped … showers of earth, mud and splinters came hurtling in on top of us. Every minute we fully expected to receive a whole one all to ourselves. There was a feeling of relief each time the spasm finished and we plucked up enough courage to joke about it. It was fortunate for us that he did not try a sprinkling of Shrapnel, as we had no head-cover of any sort.'

Overhead protection of a roof covered by earth for a trench is essential to protect the soldiers from artillery shells which are timed to explode above the target. These air-burst shells are particularly lethal when they spray hundreds of Shrapnel balls like a massive shotgun cartridge.

Soldiers at the receiving end of a barrage would have been deafened, dazed and disoriented. With an artillery barrage often the prelude to an infantry attack defenders would have to be ready to quite literally fight for their lives at any moment. They would also have been traumatised by seeing their comrades killed or hideously wounded. The artillery devastated Zandvoorde as Lieutenant the Honourable Reggie Wyndham 1/LG recalled:

'The village of Zanvoorden (sic) behind us is practically destroyed by the German shells. The church is riddled.'

At about this time Lord Tweedmouth described the after-effect of artillery: 'A quiet night but shelling in the morning and Jack Johnsons gave their attentions to the village. We watched them bursting about 150 yards from our farm. I went round the trenches in the evening and saw where they had burst. They make a hole 6 feet deep and big enough to put a cart in.'

Makeshift trenches were no match for high explosive shells nicknamed Jack Johnsons. Lord Tweedmouth also commented on the nauseating stench from rotting cow carcases.

Nearby heavy fighting was taking place at La Bassée and at Arras. By the evening of 25 October

'those that survived were in a state of extreme exhaustion both mental and physical … human endurance was nearly at the breaking point.'

At 20.30 hours Germans attacked the Kruiseik trenches south of the Menin Road which were being held by two companies of the 2nd Battalion Scots Guards and the King's Company of the 1st Grenadier Guards. Captain Payner of 2nd Battalion Scots Guards wrote:

'Our trenches were tremendously shelled all day, some of the trenches being blown in; Drummond and Kemble, being buried in their trench, had to be dug out. We noticed masses of troops advancing on our trenches. Some got as far as our trenches and were shot down, others lay in front calling out, "We surrender," and, "Don't shoot; we are Allies," and, "Where is Captain Payner G Company?" Parties got through the line on my right and left and commenced firing at us from behind. We shot at and silenced all these. Fresh lots kept coming on.

'After renewed shelling the following morning the assault renewed in earnest. The British trenches were not fit for purpose and those defenders who had not been killed or buried alive were trying to keep their rifles and machine guns free from sand, soil and debris. Germans who had infiltrated behind the trench line shouted, "Retire! Retire!"'

The line for several miles was in disorder.

In the intense fighting Lieutenant the Lord Gerald Richard Grosvenor, Lord Hugh's half-brother, was among several other officers who were badly wounded and 'in the darkness of the night fell into the enemy's hands'. It is presumed that a head wound rendered Lord Gerald incapacitated. His war record shows that the injury caused a permanent disability to his right eye. He was held at Crefeld before being moved to Münster and eventually interned in the Netherlands. Whilst recuperating Lord Gerald was promoted Captain on 18 October 1915 and repatriated to England on 23 September 1918. Lord Gerald remained on the Reserve list until reaching the age limit of 'liability to recall' on 14 July 1924. He lived near Whitchurch in Shropshire until he died on 10 December 1940 aged 66. Although only a mile or so away Lord Hugh never found out that Gerald had been wounded and had become a prisoner of war.

Major General Capper personally led a counterattack on the night of 25 October at Kruiseke and restored the line, as well as capturing nearly 200 German prisoners. Capper's actions were described by a fellow officer:

'He wasn't brave, he simply did not know what fear meant … One day when I had spoken of the risk he was running, he turned on me almost fiercely, "I consider it to be the duty of an officer in this war to be killed" he said.'

The military historian Richard Olsen summed up Capper's impact:

'There can be little doubt that the steadfastness of the 7th Division under Capper's inspirational leadership was absolutely critical to the avoidance of defeat and to the ultimate success at Ypres.'

With exceptional and uncompromising commanders such as Major General Capper, delivering pre-war Staff College training and leading by example in combat operations, it is understandable that the officers of 1914 would fight to the end and never give up. It was simply not in their nature to admit defeat. Almost inevitably luck ran out for the heroic Tommy Capper on 27 September 1915 when he was killed in action. He lies buried at Lillers Communal Cemetery near Bethune.

On 26 October, following a 36 hour artillery bombardment, two massive infantry assaults drove the 7th Division from the Kruiseke position. As the British soldiers started to withdraw

'the bombardment continued and there was an ominous trickle of men to the rear; men who were wounded; men who had been blown out of their trenches; men looking for the remains of their units; men whose rifles no longer worked because of sand clogging the mechanism; men exhausted and shocked by nights and days of fighting.'

In his diary for 26 October Haig wrote:

'When a report reaches me that the 7th Division which is holding the line from Gheluvelt to Zandvoorde is giving way I send a staff officer to find out whether they are being attacked by infantry or whether they are merely leaving their trenches on account of shell fire. He reports several Battalions in great disorder passing back though our 1st Brigade … I rode out about 3 pm to see what was going on, and was astounded at the terror-stricken men coming back. Still there were units in the division which stuck to their trenches.'

There must have been a widespread sense of crisis and impending disaster. On the same day French warned Lord Kitchener of the shortage of artillery ammunition and was told to economise. Lack of effective artillery support would have a critical impact on the ability of the Life Guards to defend Zandvoorde ridge. The apparent lack of shells for the guns was an issue of national importance. It was a commonly held belief that industry was not producing enough war materiel for the troops at the front. Even Rudyard Kipling alluded to this in his epitaph *Batteries out of Ammunition*:

'If any mourn us in the workshop, say
We died because the shift kept holiday.'

Unlike France and Germany Morgan Crofton reported: 'British industries are practically at normal strength.'

Lack of artillery support was exacerbated by a lack of serviceable machine guns. A cavalry regiment should have had two Maxims at this stage in the war, giving a Brigade a total of six, in Lord Anglesey's History of British Cavalry: 'Because of a shortage of spare parts on 26 October … 7th Cavalry Brigade had only three guns left.' The 10th (Prince of Wales's Own) Royal Hussars from the 6th Cavalry Brigade had been holding the Zandvoorde ridge for

Four casualties from the 10th Hussars – a knighted Captain lies next to a Lieutenant, a Lance Corporal and a Trooper. Captain Sir Frank S. D. Rose 2nd Bart., Lieutenant C. R. Turner, Lance Corporal J. Waugh and Private R. S. MacKenzie. (*M. J. McBride*)

four days. There are four Commonwealth War Graves in the graveyard of St Bartholomew church in Zandvoorde. The church was destroyed in the war, but four Hussars were buried in the churchyard.

A few days later the battlefield had changed so much that those who died would get a hurried battlefield burial in unmarked mass graves. Holding the Zandvoorde ridge would have been uncomfortable in the extreme, a test of anyone's endurance to breaking point. The ground turns to mud easily and the so-called 'trenches' would have been water-logged. Without proper entrenching tools and entrenching materiel it would not have been possible to improve the position by deepening the holes and creating dugouts with proper overhead protection against artillery. The iconic steel helmet, or 'tin hat', would not be issued for some time to come. The soldiers had no protection from shot or shell. Frequent requests in Lord Hugh's letters for warm clothing and a neck muffler indicate that their issued uniform offered them no protection from the elements either.

Although the British trenches during the battle were abominable they were officially described by the Germans thus: 'The enemy had prepared a series of lines of strong trenches covered by an extensive system of artificial obstacles.' That description of the state of the British frontline would have amused the average Tommy sat in his muddy excuse for a trench.

The Zandvoorde trenches were a known death-trap. They would have been cold, wet, muddy and frightening places in which to serve in October 1914.

'The trenches were not well regulated but pits dug in the sandy soil each holding around a dozen men. They were short sections far apart with no communications laterally or from behind. Relief was during the hours of darkness with no time, opportunity or tools to make them better. Dispositions followed the contours of the ridge with trenches susceptible to artillery fire with incoming artillery averaging 120 shells per day and casualties were continuous.'

As the

'generals believed a war of movement would recur in the spring … there was no need to waste thought or energy improving temporary positions.'

In the book 'Horsemen in No Man's Land', it was stated that the cavalry soldier was ill-equipped for trench warfare. Whereas the infantryman could carry his equipment in purpose designed webbing pouches and a haversack, the cavalryman simply had to fill the pockets of his greatcoat or wrap everything up in a blanket roll and 'soldier on'. It must have made their time in the trenches even more miserable than ever.

Without adequate sandbags it would not have been possible to create a bullet-proof parapet with loopholes to allow soldiers protection against fire from their front. They would have to literally stick their heads over the top to observe. Trench periscopes would not have been widely available in 1914.

The design of fighting trenches later in the war resembled a zig-zag rather than a straight channel. These traverses were to prevent a single shell killing everyone in a long straight trench. Later designs of trench connected the front line fighting trench, or fire trench, to the rear with shallower communication trenches to allow soldiers to walk to and from the front without exposing themselves to enemy fire. In fact the Zandvoorde 'trenches' were described as being little more than a string of unconnected holes. Worse than that, it has been commented how poorly they had been sited. Following the crest around the village they were in full view of the enemy artillery observation officers.

How men coped with the situation in Zandvoorde trenches remains a mystery to later generations. Perhaps they were kept going by that combination of comradeship, regimental pride, ingrained discipline and a simple determination not to give in that is the hallmark of the British soldier. They would hang on and give the enemy a pasting when he came into view. There was no glory in such a situation, no glory in this kind of life, but these men gained a kind of glory, simply by enduring it. In that same area the British Official History noted that

> 'the line that stood between the British Empire and ruin was composed of tired haggard and unshaven men, many in uniforms that were little more than rags. But they had their guns, rifles and bayonets.'

The bayonet is the bladed weapon attached to the end of a rifle and used for close-quarter combat. It is the iconic symbol for the infantryman. In September 1914 the 5th Royal Dragoon Guards were promised 500 bayonets before being issued with a paltry 25. Corporal of Horse Lloyd stated that at this time all of the 3rd Cavalry Division had actually been issued with bayonets. It appears that whether a cavalryman at this point in the war was issued with a bayonet, or not, was something of a lottery.

The bayonet had some use as a makeshift entrenching tool in the absence of anything better. Cavalrymen unused to the bayonet soon realized the importance of keeping the locking mechanisms clean or 'the result was that rapid fire caused the bayonet to fall off, generally on the wrong side of the parapet. The owner had to retrieve it in an operation apt to be unhealthy.'

The worst things to endure in the Zandvoorde position though was the artillery shells bringing random death or wounding and the fear of a sniper's bullet in the head to the unwary. Being under threat from an enemy sniper was extremely stressful. Snipers were experts in camouflage, fieldcraft, observation and marksmanship. Morgan Crofton described the situation:

'The sniper hit another Blue (Royal Horse Guardsman) bang through the forehead. The body was dragged passed me with great difficulty as it was very heavy … His friend covered his head with a Macintosh sheet, but as he was being pulled along it fell over, and I have never seen such a look of surprised horror as the poor dead man's face had as he passed me.'

Some soldiers even tried to draw the fire from enemy snipers:

'Several humourists in The Blues entertained themselves in putting their caps on the end of their rifles and holding them in the air, where they were at once hit by the watchful sniper. This first caused some hilarity but it became very unpopular, since the bullet after piercing the cap often went ricocheting down some other trench some distance off, causing some dismay amongst those who were not taking part in the game.'

Although this account was dismissed by Crofton as the infantile antics of bored soldiers it was to become part of the counter-sniper tactics as the war continued. *Papier-mach*é dummy heads of Allied soldiers were skilfully produced to draw fire from concealed enemy snipers. These heads became very realistic indeed and some even had burning cigarettes placed in their mouths operated by a rubber tube. Once the enemy sniper had fired his shot at the target head a periscope was put behind it to line up the entry and exit holes to pinpoint the spot where the sniper was. A quick telephone call to an artillery battery on standby would then bring down a barrage on the enemy's position.

At long range a sniper could be of nuisance value as in this account when Corporal of Horse Lloyd visited Brigadier General Kavanagh's Headquarters which was a lone house at the foot of Zandvoorde ridge:

'On entering, as I was passing through the door, I heard the double crack of a German rifle away on the ridge behind me and a bullet rattled among the tiles of the roof. I thought this is a lively place for the headquarters of a general, but I was not there to criticise what he was pleased to make his temporary abode, so I went in and got to business.'

The 'double crack' is the experience one gets being fired upon, often called, 'crack-and-thump'. The 'crack' is the sound barrier being broken as the bullet travels past at supersonic speed; the 'thump' is the sound from the muzzle of the firearm which reaches the target later as it travels at the speed of sound, i.e. slower than the bullet.

'Having completed my business … I went out again through the door. Again the sniper fired and again his bullet hit the roof. The occupants of the billet could never account for his bad shooting, any more than they could locate his position. Though most persistent day after day, he never managed to cause a casualty.'

In the German High Command final preparations were being made to attack Zandvoorde. On 27 October Lieutenant General von Falkenhayn decided to create a new attacking formation called Army Group Fabeck which would spearhead the attack towards Ypres. This battle group under General von Fabeck would consist of II Bavarian and the XV Corps, 6th Bavarian Reserve Division, the 26th Würtenberg Division plus all of the artillery which the Sixth Army could muster for the attack on 30 October.

In his letter dated 27 October Lord Hugh wrote:

'My Darling, I am afraid I haven't written for some time but ever since the 19th with the exception of one day we have been hard at it fighting most of the time. On the 20th we had to take up a line in front of one infantry and dig ourselves into trenches where we remained under heavy shell fire for the morning, how our horses escaped I cant (sic) imagine as the shells were bursting bang over them all of the time. Corpl Cram was wounded, several horses hit and a few killed. We then went back behind the infantry line and waited a long time doing nothing before we got the order to go into billets some way off, in the meanwhile we watched a battle which was going on in inky darkness, the scene more or less lighted up by the blazing farms which had been set alight by shells.'

At about this time it appears that Lord Hugh's horses were withdrawn to safety and effectively his squadron became proto-infantry. A dismounted cavalryman's first concern is always for his horse – his 'pal'. It must have been a huge relief for Lord Hugh to know that his horses were safely out of harm's way.

The relentless military bureaucracy was something which Lord Hugh was evidently bored with:

'I have only a few minutes more as I am being bothered with orders and papers and things so will you send this letter around if you think anyone would like to see it.'

Again Lord Hugh requested more comforts from home:

'Will you send me cigarettes and a small warm muffler brown for choice and Simmonds tobacco also 2 pipes.'

Lord Hugh's concern for the welfare of farm animals caught up in the conflict was apparent:

'The saddest part of this war is to see so many farms burning and the wretched cattle, sheep and pigs wandering about, one comes across farms completely deserted by their owners with cows tied up in the sheds. I always let them out if possible and the men milk them when they have the time. My Squadron is doing well and the horses are keeping going fairly well, all Combermere horses still alive. Bonner is very fit. Just got your letter I was delighted about Harry it is splendid'.

'Combermere' was Combermere Barracks which was renamed in honour of Lord Combermere, the Colonel of 1/LG until 1865.

Touchingly Lord Hugh still had his family in mind:

'Gerald and John must be having fun. Bless you Darling. Love to everybody. We are all flourishing and I am enjoying myself the work is hard but the news is good so it doesn't matter. Your Hugh. No news of brother Gerry but they have been fighting hard.'

'Brother Gerry', Captain Gerald Richard Grosvenor, 2nd Battalion Scots Guards, had been wounded and captured two days before.

At Zandvoorde Gerry Worsley's machine-gun section was positioned right in the front line. In fact the Household Cavalry Memorial stands on the site where Worsley was buried next to his machine-gun post. Paul Cornish comments that

'some very basic rules were being ignored with the tactical deployment of machine guns in the first year of the war. Prominent among these was the fact that the firepower of machine guns is hugely more effective in enfilade, i.e. when fired from a flanking position, than when it is aimed directly into the enemy's front line.'

It would appear that Worsley's machine guns were right in the middle of the Zandvoorde ridge trench. Cornish continues that

'it has been recorded that a pre-war machine-gun officer upon requesting orders for his guns was told to "take the damned things to the flank and hide 'em" by his superior. In fact, given the tactical precepts of the time, there was no better position for these weapons than concealed on the flank of their parent formation.'

Neither Worsley nor Lord Hugh chose the location where they fought and died; it is open to speculation if the outcome of the battle would have been materially different had the trenches been better sited and the machine guns concealed in an enfilade position. Armchair generals have the gift of hindsight – the soldiers who fought like lions cannot be blamed for the situation in which they found themselves.

Although Lord Hugh was out of the trenches he was well aware of the dire situation:

'My Darling, Just a line to thank you for the matches and the other useful things. I should like cigarettes so much. We are now in reserve trenches behind the fighting line as we had more than our share of the fighting the other day. I have just seen Peter Poole marching by with the remnants of his Battalion they have 3 officers and 250 men left out of a full Battalion a colonel and 2 subalterns they have had a rotten time and so have many others but the Germans had worse.'

Peter Poole was a Lieutenant in 1/RWF and his battalion had beaten off two attacks on 20 October 1914 at Zonnebecke. The following day the attack intensified,

'but (it) held out until 4 pm when their trenches had been wholly annihilated and retirement became necessary'.

Astonishingly, defective ammunition had been issued (the brass cartridge cases were slightly oversized) and the Fusiliers had to force the bolts open with a sharp tug and, if that failed, they would have had to ground the butt and stomp on the bolt handle or bash it with a heavy object. The presence of sand and the absence of gun oil exacerbated the problem. The malfunctioning of rifles was of such importance that it even featured in Sir Douglas Haig's diary: 'Rifles jammed owing to mud and soil and no opportunity for cleaning and oiling.' In one week of fighting the 1/RWF lost 864 men and 23 officers. On 25 October the Battalion was pulled out of the line for a brief period of rest.

'I am trying to get news of Gerry but I can't find out yet the fighting has been terrific around here for the last week and so far we have been successful and look like continuing to be. Jerry Markham is I hear badly wounded. I saw a wonderful sight the other day a German aeroplane hit by one of our shells it burst into flames in the air and came gracefully to earth. It is the second one to be brought down in this neighbourhood.'

On 26 October Corporal of Horse Lloyd echoed Lord Hugh's account:

'At 6 am we were ordered to saddle up preparatory to changing our position. At 10 am the order was cancelled. While standing to a German plane was brought down by our artillery. This was the first time we saw that sort of thing happen.'

Lord Hugh continued:

'Dick Sutton has gone home wounded, write to him about the pony he must have forgotten it. Tell Eric Gerry is awfully well and so popular in the Regiment. Everyone says he is so changed he works all days and produces food from every conceivable corner of his clothes which are decidedly dirty as he upset a dish of bacon into his lap the other day. We expect to be joined by the Composite soon they will probably be amalgamated into this Brigade as it is impossible to get reserves for both lots. I hope they will work. It will be much nicer to be together and I will still keep my squadron. We work like nothing on earth now dirty and grimy. I had a good wash yesterday and at last had a good sleep in a potato shed on some straw. Gerry snores. It will be most amazing to see the accounts of this battle in the papers if it ever gets in.

'I am sending you on a letter from Sybil it is a shame to laugh at her but one can't help smiling at it. Will you send me a night cap muffler you know the things you can either put it on your head or wear it as a muffler they are most useful. The men will be grateful for your socks and drawers. Shirts will be the next thing they will want and they should not have collars on. It is hard to collect news here

away from one's own little area. The line is such a vast length. Hugh
Dawnay is now in command of the 2nd Algy Teck has gone on the
King of the Belgians staff. The poor old 2nd have caught it badly. Sam
Ashton, Robin Duff. Young Palmer Pemberton killed. Lyn Fergusson
wounded. Alpy Strutt sick. Montgomerie. Altogether in this brigade
we have 19 officers killed, wounded or sick. Some very slight, but all
away. Jaff the vet is very ill. Jazeka slightly wounded and sick. He had
a shrapnel bullet stuck in his lip which made him gobble more than
ever. Romy Hamilton wounded in the arm. We are all very well and all
bored to death with infantry work in the trenches, it looks as if we are
going to do a good deal of it.'

'Dick Sutton' was Captain Sir R. Sutton Bart who was listed as wounded in
the Life Guards War Records; 'Hugh Dawnay' was the Honourable Hugh
Dawnay 2/LG who was killed on 6 November 1914 and 'The poor old 2nd'
was the 2nd Regiment of Life Guards, 2/LG. Lord Hugh's comments are
prophetic, indeed there was to be four years of trench warfare.

'Try and see Phillip Brocklehurst he will tell you all he saw but
unluckily he was shot the first big day we had and early at that. The
General is a ripper and so nice to all of us and as brave as a lion. Neill
the brigade major received a bullet through his behind the same day
as Brocklehurst was hit. We have always had lots of food and I haven't
tackled the soap squares yet we are keeping them for Germany.'

Lord Hugh obviously still hoped to ride victorious into Germany:

'There is an infernal sniper shooting at us as I write this in a dirty
cottage and we can't locate him. Close Brooks is dying to go out and
hunt for him, but it is hardly worthwhile as he is hidden probably up
some tree and probably dressed as a peasant. The search party has
already been out after him without success.
                    Bless you Darling
                    Love to everybody
                    Your Own Hugh

Will you send Cox £40 to pay my mess bills. He won't pay as he says I am £14 overdrawn dirty dog.

I have lost the good chestnut he went away to the base and I shan't see him again but I have now one of Phillip's.

Please send mufflers, cigarettes and tobacco.'

The conditions in these cottages and farm buildings were far from ideal as Morgan Crofton reported:

'Went out … to have a look at the country round the farm which has now been dignified by the name of 'Mud Farm'. I must say it lives up to its name, a more filthy place I have never seen!'

Corporal of Horse Lloyd described Mud Farm as:

'Mud, cold, deep and sticky was over everything and in everything. It took half an hour to walk two hundred yards in any direction.'

Zandvoorde 'Remains of village'. (*Private Collection*)

St Bartholomew's church, Zaandvoorde village today. (*M. J. McBride*)

Zandvoorde was an obvious prize for the Imperial German Army. The ridge was an essential precursor to advancing on Ypres and beyond. This was no surprise to 1/LG. According to their war diary on 28 October intelligence had been received from an enemy radio intercept that an attack was due on the following morning:

'Reliable information has again been received that the German 27th Reserve Corps will attack at 5.30 am Kruseik-Zandvoorde position.'

On 29 October Lord Hugh wrote home to Lady Grosvenor for the last time,

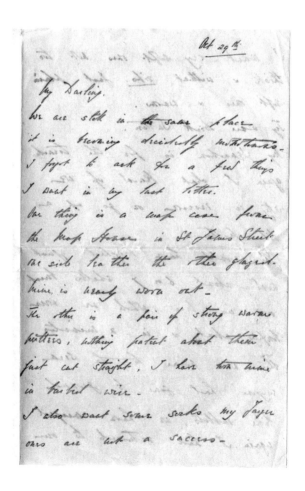

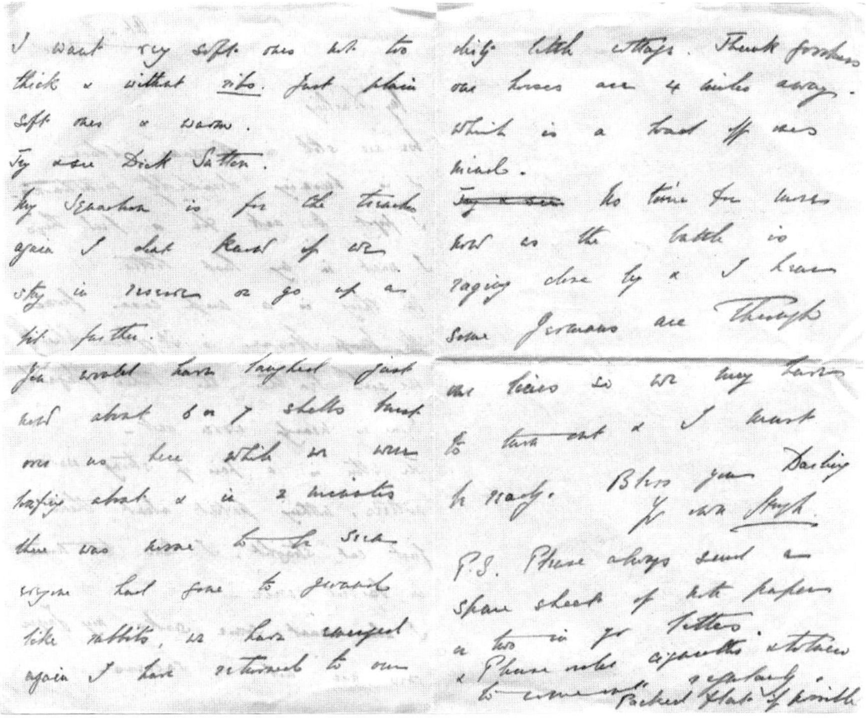
I want very soft ones but too thick & without ribs. Just plain soft ones & warm.
Try & see Dick Sutton.
My Squadron is for the trenches again I don't know if we stay in reserve or go up a bit further.
You would have laughed just now about 6 or 7 shells burst on us here while we were loafing about & in 2 minutes there was none to be seen everyone had gone to ground like rabbits, we have emerged again I have returned to our

dirty little cottage. Thank goodness our horses are 4 miles away. Which is a load off ones mind.
~~Try & see~~ No time for more now as the battle is raging close by & I hear some Germans are through our lines so we may have to turn out & I want to be ready. Bless you Darling
Yr own Hugh.

P.S. Please always send a spare sheet of note paper & two in yr letters.
& Please send cigarettes [illegible] separately [illegible] to come [illegible] Pocket Flask if possible.

'My Darling, We are still in the same place it is becoming decidedly monotonous. I forgot to ask for a few things I want in my last letter.

One thing is a map case from the Map House in St James Street one side leather the other glazed. Mine is already worn out.

The other is a pair of strong warm puttees, nothing patent about them just cut straight. I have torn mine on barbed wire.

I also want some socks my Jäger ones are not a success. I want very soft ones but not too thick and without ribs. Just plain soft ones and warm.

Try and see Dick Sutton.

My Squadron is for the trenches again I don't know if we stay in reserve or go up a bit further.

You should have laughed just now about 6 or 7 shells burst on us here while we were loafing about and in 2 minutes there was no-one to be seen everyone had gone to ground like rabbits, we have emerged again and I have returned to our dirty little cottage. Thank goodness our horses are 4 miles away which is a load off ones mind.'

It was mid-November before a Veterinary Officer 'shocked at the state of our horses, particularly those which had been slightly wounded and whose wounds were now ugly running sores owing to lack of proper protection from the poisonous mud, decided to evacuate them. He purloined the services of three troopers and despatched them and forty sick or wounded horses on a train bound for the British Veterinary Hospital near Dunkirk. A month later the three soldiers returned to their parent unit. Having delivered their charges to the Veterinary Hospital they allegedly made their return journey on foot due to the railway lines being severed. They told tales of being co-opted into various units *en route* and heroic military actions. It was only four years later that one of the three soldiers admitted that they had sold the horses to local Belgian traders for meat or farm work and spent a month in Dunkirk on the proceeds.

Hugh continued 'No time for more now as the battle is raging close by and I hear some Germans are through our lines so we may have to turn out and I must be ready.

Bless you Darling

Your Own Hugh

P.S. Please always send a spare sheet of note paper or two in your letters and please note, cigarettes and tobacco to come out regularly packed flat if possible.'

Lord Hugh's letters are conversational jumping from topic to topic almost as a stream of consciousness. Always demonstrating care for his soldiers and his beloved horses; often poignant about the effects of the war on his comrades and civilians; eternally optimistic of a positive outcome; requesting comforts; and expressing his love and devotion to his wife and sons.

Lord Hugh ended his letter,

'No time for more now as the battle is raging close by and I hear some
Germans are through our lines so we may have to turn out and I must
be ready.'

It can be imagned that he had to finish the letter hurriedly as news got
around that the British line had been broken.

The British line had indeed been broken a few miles away at Gheluvelt.
The small town lay on the Menin to Ypres road and the Germans threw
a massive attack against the sparse numbers of BEF at 05.30 hours on 29
October. By midday the Germans had broken the line. There was nothing
more than a few scattered British units left between Gheluvelt and Ypres.
There was no concerted defence at all to stop the Germans. However at
14.30 hours, in one of the most heroic feats of arms of the war, the 2nd
Battalion Royal Worcesters retook Gheluvelt in a bayonet charge and
stopped the attack.

In a cruel twist of fate this action at Gheluvelt caused the 6th Cavalry
Brigade to remain committed in the support *role* so they were unable to relieve
the 7th Cavalry Brigade which was manning the Zandvoorde trenches on 30
October when the attack occurred. As the machine gun of the Life Guards
was unserviceable Lord Worsley and his RHG machine-gun section could
not be released from the frontline. On being told that his section would need
to stay put Lord Worsley characteristically grinned, laughed and said it was
'all in a day's work'. He wrote home,

'I am still in the trenches …. Last night was the most miserable I have
ever spent …. it poured and blew all night.'

According to the 1/LG war diary:

'Zandvoorde Regiment should have been relieved by 6th Brigade at
dusk, but during afternoon 6th Brigade were called out to support
infantry on left, so Regiment remained in trenches. C Squadron and 2
Troops of D from Reserve relieved 1½ Squadron Royal Horse Guards
in trenches. At 05.30 hours German forces attack British line along

Menin Road causing massive casualties to the first Battalions of the Coldstream and Grenadier Guards. At 15.00 hours the line is held.'

There is reason to believe that the attack on Zandvoorde had originally been planned for 29 October to coincide with that on Kruiseke, but a delay in the arrival of the XV German Army Corps resulted in its postponement till the following day. The expected reinforcements arrived during the night of 29 October and, with all plans in place, the attack took place at daybreak on the following morning. The increasing tempo and force of the German attacks coincided with the arrival of their Kaiser. He was to remain for the next five days in anticipation of a breakthrough and a victorious advance through Ypres.

General Fabeck issued the following order exhorting his soldiers to attack the British vigorously on the following day:

'Tomorrow ... we are to attack the British around Zandvoorde ... and then push on to Ypres. This breakthrough is of decisive importance for the outcome of the war. Therefore we shall and must be victorious! His Majesty the Kaiser trusts that each will try his utmost to do his duty. We shall make sure that we justify this trust. Brave and undaunted we are going to attack the British, Indians, Canadians, Moroccans and all such rabble. The enemy is becoming worn out and recently, whenever we have gone for them energetically, they have surrendered in large numbers. So let us go forward with God for our Kaiser and our beloved German Fatherland!'

General Major Konrad Kraft von Dellmensingen ordered his officers to lead from the front:

'every commander is personally to ensure, including by example, that he is so engaged that the attack will be conducted with the utmost power.'

The Germans had seen the British withdraw at Mons and Le Cateau and there was every confidence that they would do the same at Zandvoorde.

'One factor in the case, however, had been overlooked, or at least underrated viz. the indomitable tenacity of the British soldier in the face of difficulties. The stonewall resistance put up by our war-worn Army Corps must have been a source of equal astonishment and exasperation to Berlin.'

The last time most of Lord Hugh's men saw friendly troops was during the night of 29 October when a ration party made a delivery.

'It became known about three o'clock that afternoon that the Regiment could not be relieved that night, as the 6th Cavalry Brigade, which should have furnished the relief, was away supporting the infantry. This gave birth to a fresh adventure in the shape of a ration party to the line after dark ... never have I seen such a hopeless mix-up as was made of the attempt to get rations into the line on Zandvoorde ridge on the night of 29th October.'

The rations consisted of biscuits, corned beef (bully beef) and tinned milk in bulk. The consignment had not been broken down into smaller loads which would have made distribution easier and safer.

'Progress up the side of the hill was slow and language flowed hot and strong. On reaching the village we came under fire, but we all too fed up to care, so without halting we pushed on over the brow of the hill and kept to the road. A few yards down the road a nasty spurt from a machine gun caused us to make a dive for the ditch by the roadside, where we sprawled among the boxes and sacks till the firing stopped. If the rations had been properly divided up we could have run along the back of the trenches and handed them over ourselves in no time.'

Instead, after an hour's wait, soldiers from the trenches emerged to drag the bulk rations away. How they managed to split up what was to be, for most of them, their last meal is not known. The Gordon Highlanders had been relieved from their trenches and were lying down a short way behind the line in case of attack. They only had a few short hours to wait. The sound of vehicles and horses on the move was heard by the Household Cavalrymen during the night. This was the prelude to the German onslaught as they manoeuvred their heavy artillery into place and their troops filed into their assault positions. The German High Command's analysis of the battle exaggerated the strength of the Allied manpower and weaponry perhaps as a way of explaining why their breakthrough was unsuccessful. The British review of the German version of events noted:

'The fact seems to be that the Germans cannot understand defeat in war except on the premise that the victor had superiority of numbers …'

The logical German Supreme Headquarters believed wrongly that behind the British line were reserves. One of their aims of the attack on 30 October was to,

'compel the use of these reserves, or at least dissuade the enemy commanders from moving them to other sectors.'

It would be unconceivable to the German military mind for the British to contemplate holding ground with just a single defensive line.

Chapter 11

30 October 1914

When the hammer fell on the Zandvoorde position on 30 October 1914 it was an awful demonstration of a storm of artillery fire on poorly prepared trenches followed by a massed infantry attack.

On a grassy knoll before the village of Zandvoorde the Household Cavalry in their new *role* as infantry were positioned in trenches just south of the Zandvoorde-Tenbrielen Road. These rudimentary trenches, badly sited on the downward slopes of the ridge, were in full view of an approaching enemy. The left flank of the 7th Cavalry Brigade consisted of C Squadron 2nd Life Guards commanded by Captain Alexander Vandeleur from the 1st Battalion of the Royal Welch Fusiliers' position to the road. On the other side of the road was C Squadron of the 1/LG commanded by Captain Lord Hugh Grosvenor and the RHG machine-gun section of Lieutenant Lord Worsley. The Squadron had a view of all that was likely to approach them but this was counter-balanced by their position on the open high ground being exposed to enemy eyes. Lord Hugh was aware of the danger presented by his squadron's isolated position and contacted brigade headquarters asking for artillery fire to protect his flanks but, before the support could be effected, the Germans opened a devastating bombardment on the position using all 260 heavy artillery guns of the 6th Army. The enemy artillery consisted of eight batteries of mortars, 20 battalions of heavy field howitzers (each of three batteries) and a 305 mm calibre coastal defence mortar for good measure.

This was followed by the German 39th Division plus three Jäger Battalions hurling themselves against the thin line of the Household Cavalry stretched along the ridge.

'At the moment of the final attack the 7th Cavalry Brigade had been in the trenches for three days and nights, under a ceaseless shellfire … in the case of the machine-gun section of the Blues, under Lord Worsley, that period doubled.'

Kaiser Wilhelm II

'had come forward to view the attack as he had known many of the Household officers in pre-war days.'

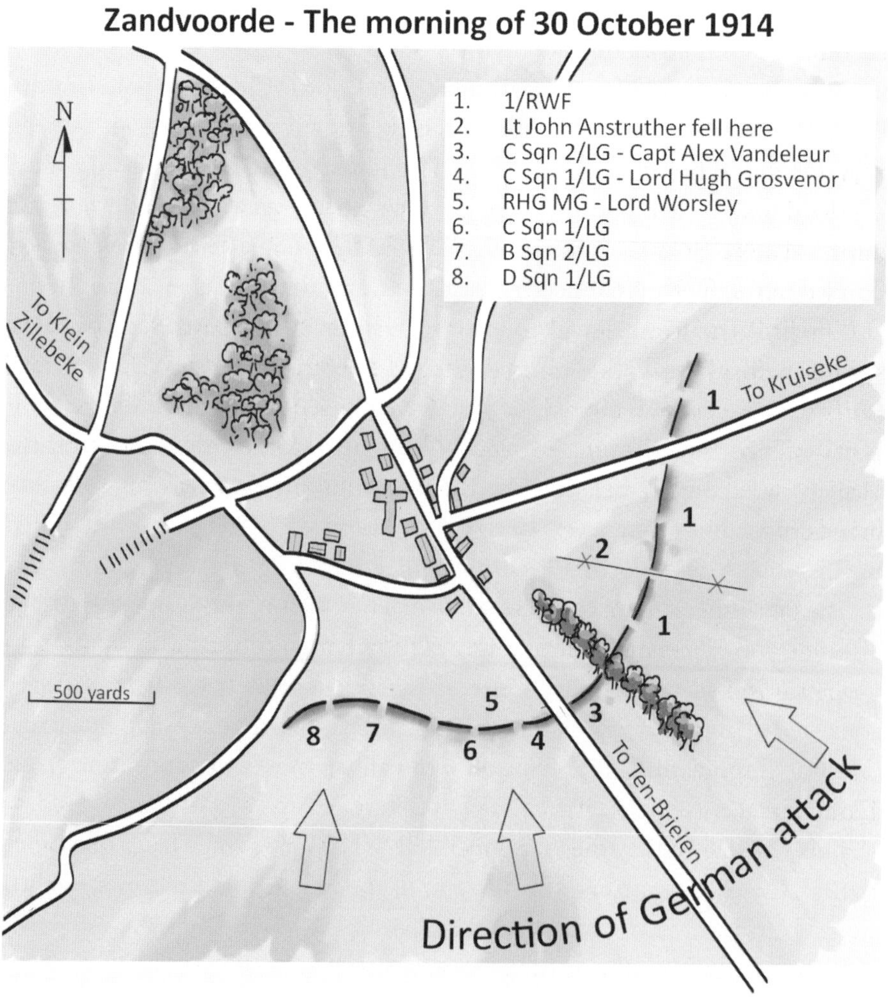
Zandvoorde - The morning of 30 October 1914
1. 1/RWF
2. Lt John Anstruther fell here
3. C Sqn 2/LG - Capt Alex Vandeleur
4. C Sqn 1/LG - Lord Hugh Grosvenor
5. RHG MG - Lord Worsley
6. C Sqn 1/LG
7. B Sqn 2/LG
8. D Sqn 1/LG
N
To Klein Zillebeke
To Kruiseke
To Ten-Brielen
500 yards
1
1
2
1
3
4
5
6
7
8
Direction of German attack

Map 5: Map showing the positions of the Household Cavalry at Zandvoorde on 30 October 1914. (*David Parkland*)

The German plan was for a set of batteries to open up with three salvoes to signal that the bombardment was to begin. This was to be at first 'gunner light' – the time when artillery observers can make out their targets at battlefield ranges. The poor visibility meant that it was 08.00 hours before the bombardment started and 09.00 hours before the infantry started their advance.

The Germans reported that:

'The advance was far from easy. The battlefield was fundamentally flat, offering good fields of fire.'

It was also crisscrossed by streams making progress slow. It is recorded that Oberst Kreyenberg attempted to motivate his troops by ordering the Regimental drummers to beat the drums for the assault and blow the appropriate bugle calls. Additionally he ordered the Regimental band to play martial music further to encourage the men.

The final enemy assault was executed with courage, but without tactical skill or field-craft, leading to significant waste of life. One of the German units participating in the assault was Infantry Regiment 136. Most of this unit's officers were killed 'due to the obstinate defence being put up by the British defenders'. According to the Marquess of Anglesey some of the attackers were

'the flower of the youth of Germany, middle and upper-class students, under military-age volunteers, hardly trained but burning with patriotism'.

Although some of the Germans were experienced soldiers from Jäger Battalions it was apparent that many were poorly trained and poorly led on that day. Nearby at Messines Trooper Albert Whitelock of The Bays recalled that

'the German infantry seemed to wander forward not knowing where to go, while their guns kept firing, not seeming to care whether they hit friend or foe.'

With the ferocity of the artillery bombardment and the lack of protection offered by makeshift trenches it can be inferred that many of C Squadron would have become casualties. The rounds were Shrapnel (airburst) and high explosive. The former would have exploded above the trenches raining deadly Shrapnel balls on the defenders. The latter would have buried into the ground before exploding and creating massive craters.

Farrar-Hockley summarises the entire battle:

'The high explosive fell and blew and blasted amongst the squadrons, some of whose trenches were dug in echelon across the forward slopes, the remainder running west across the valley to the bank of the Ypres-Comines canal. Those on the slope of Zandvoorde hill fared worst and the 400 men, the sum of two regiments, who had stood to at dawn had been reduced to 320 by 8 o'clock. The brigade commander then saw a mass of Germans approaching – two regiments of the 39th Division and three battalions of Jäger. He decided that his regiments must be moved back before they were overwhelmed and sent these orders to the two commanding officers, but the two squadrons on the slopes and the section of machine guns could not get out; the enemy guns had already fired on the target of their trenches many times and the moment they were seen in the open, Shrapnel was added to high explosive. They were annihilated.'

Although the artillery bombardment was the most intense the British had ever experienced up to this point it is clear that by no means all of Lord Hugh's comrades was incapacitated by it. The defenders were aware that the previous day the Germans had broken the British line nearby at Gheluvelt but heroic actions that day saved the situation. Maybe, just maybe, they could stop the Germans. The defenders of the Zandvoorde trenches knew how vitally important it was to deny, or at least delay, the Germans from taking the high ground from a strategic perspective:

'We all knew there was nothing behind us, and when the attack came, if we did not stop it nothing could.'

Lord Hugh would have been motivated to fight to the end with his friends and comrades including Captain Alexander Vandeleur on his left and Lieutenant Lord Worsley on his right. It could be that with a millennium of service his mind was enflamed by his noble lineage. Maybe, being steeped in military history, Lord Hugh drew inspiration from Thermopylae to Mons. Being a product of the post-Victorian officer class Lord Hugh felt it was his patriotic duty to King and Empire. Pragmatically he could have been motivated by fighting for his soldiers. One will never know.

What they would have undoubtedly known was how perilous it would be to allow the Germans to take the position as it would make the neighbouring trenches to the north-east occupied by the 1st Battalion the Royal Welch Fusiliers untenable. Linear trenches are vulnerable to fire from the side, known as enfilade fire, and the defenders of such trenches would have been wiped out by machine-gun fire.

There are several accounts of the attack from the official war diary to eye witnesses. The laconic 1/LG war diary makes grim reading:

'Zandvoorde 6am. Heavy bombardment of position opened. At 7.30am position was attacked by large force of infantry. This attack proved successful owing to greatly superior numbers. Regiment retired in good order about 10am except C Squadron on left flank from which only about ten men got back. Remainder of Squadron missing.

Casualty list included:

Wounded:
2nd Lieutenant Lord Althorp

Missing:
Captain the Lord Hugh Grosvenor,
Captain E D F Kelly,
Lieutenant Hon Gerald Ward,
Lieutenant J Close Brooks,
100 rank and file.'

In fact the 1st Life Guards lost four officers and 62 others ranks which included 52 cavalry of the line. The 2nd Life Guards lost three officers and 12 other ranks eight of which were cavalry of the line. Finally the Royal Horse Guards machine-gun section lost two officers and 22 other ranks including 12 cavalry of the line. The names of all of the casualties are engraved on the Household Cavalry Memorial.

The perfunctory manner in which the tragic loss of so many men was described might surprise a modern reader, but as war veteran Captain Lord Ernest Hamilton laconically noted:

'The reticence of the records of the Regiments ... in the dignity with which, without any blare of trumpets, they tell the daily answer to the call of duty which balanced them ceaselessly on the edge of eternity.'

The official history states:

'The trenches, of the narrow type of the period, sited on a forward slope and easily seen by the enemy, without any form of shelter except cover from weather, were blown in whenever a heavy shell came near them, and many men were buried. It was obvious that under such a fire, a choice between annihilation or retirement was only a matter of time, and orders were issued for the second line to be manned by the supports. Nevertheless, the three or four hundred men of the Household Cavalry held out until 8 am, at which hour an infantry attack in overwhelming force – the 39th Division and the Jäger battalions – was launched against them. Orders for retirement to the second line were then issued, one of the 1st and one of the 2nd Life Guards with the Royal Horse Guards machine guns, were unfortunately cut off and annihilated, only a very few wounded being taken prisoner.'

One of the few survivors Captain the Honourable Reginald 'Reggie' Wyndham of 1/LG recalled:

'In the morning they attacked us. They shelled us hard, and one of the first shells buried Dawes all except his head and also buried my belt, pillow, glasses and haversack. Then their infantry attacked, we knocked a good few over, but the Maxim on our right ran out of ammunition and one trench on our right was driven in. We kept on firmly until our ammunition was finished. The spare box was buried by the shell which buried Dawes. In the end we had no more ammunition and they began to enfilade us from our right. Had to order Sgt Arthurs to retire from the right hand trench, and then ordered my troop to retire. Previous to this had dug Dawes out with my hands. Before we started to retire Cpl Brooks had been slightly hit in two places. We ran back to the farm, the Maxim killed Sgt Arthurs. Then after finding Clowes had left the farm, I went on, and found Dawes and Brooks. Dawes was slightly hit. We found Bussey badly wounded, but could not move him. We picked up a man of Arthurs' troop and helped him along until he dropped dead. Then when we reached the X-roads where Levigne was buried, Dawes had his leg broken by the shell-fire. The shells had been bursting over us all the way. Had to leave Dawes lying where he was. Then met Humphrey, who told me the order to retire had been signalled to me. Then met General Kavanagh who told me he wished me to retire. Then set to work to find the men. Found most of them when we got back to the horses. As we retired down the road, the Germans shelled us and Charlie Fitzmaurice was killed. Then found that my troop of twenty had 9 killed and wounded, and there were only 7 left of Arthur's troop of 26 men. Pickles Lambton was killed last night and they say that Hugh Grosvenor and all his Squadron bar Jerry Ward and a few men are missing.'

The Knightsbridge Barracks buddy of Cabby Dawes, Corporal of Horse Lloyd remembered the attack:

'A hellish bombardment broke out upon Zandvoorde ridge. Its suddenness and intensity caused us to stand still for a moment or two and gape. For upwards of an hour the ground trembled and the air was full of din. Then gradually the shelling subsided and machine-gun and rifle-fire swelled up into a roar. About 8.30 or 9 am the rifle fire grew less lively. When the order to retire was given it did not reach the main body of 'C' Squadron owing to its position being slightly detached from, and in front of the regiment. Lord Hugh Grosvenor, 'C' Squadron Leader, was not the man who would retire without orders, so they just fought it out and died where they stood.'

Although Morgan Crofton of 2/LG was not present at the battle he wrote an account shortly afterwards:

'(Captain A. M.) Vandeleur, (Captain J. F.) Todd and (Second Lieutenant J. A. St. C.) Anstruther were in the Squadron that was in the trenches when they were rushed by the Germans on Oct 30 at Zandvoorde. These trenches were perfect death traps, the supports being a mile and a half away and out of sight behind a hill. Only one man ever returned and his tale was very incoherent. He remembers hearing Anstruther call out 'Good God they've got round us' and then seeing him run out with his revolver and fall. No further news has ever been heard of Vandeleur or Todd, nor of the 70 men who composed their Squadron in the trench. It is feared that all were bayoneted. (Second Lieutenant M. W.) Graham was also with them, and he was supposed to be missing. Then one day about a month later his mother wrote to the War Office and said that her son had been at home with her for three weeks, wounded. He can give no account of what happened on that day.'

The verbatim, 'Good God they've got round us,' from Lieutenant Anstruther has a compelling authenticity as Crofton had spoken to a survivor. Lieutenant John Arnold Saint Clair Anstruther was an old Etonian and the son of Colonel Anstruther D.S.O., M.V.O. who had been the Commanding Officer of 2/LG. In one or more points it would appear that the German infantry had breached the ragged line of trenches and cut-off Lord Hugh's line of withdrawal. Several runners sent to give Lord Hugh orders to retire were shot down, thereby supporting the idea that German troops were behind the first line of trenches and had sealed the fate of the Household Cavalrymen. One wounded Life Guardsman who had been ordered to the rear before his comrades were cut off was Ernest Hook:

'There was no protection from the shelling as our trenches were on the forward slope and in full view of the enemy and although our gunners put up a great show, they were no match for Jerry's heavy stuff. We could see their infantry in great masses about 1,000 yards away. Just about then I was hit by a shell that nearly took my left arm off and my officer sent me to the rear.'

Another survivor was Hubert Bussey. At about 09.00 hours Corporal of Horse Lloyd rode towards the ridge and encountered Bussey:

'With his forehead cut open and bleeding. He was walking calmly back, smoking a cigarette, and looking for the dressing-station. Obviously he was badly shaken. I could get no information from him.'

It would be easy to surmise that the intensity of the artillery barrage stunned the defenders. Lloyd continued:

'Round the next bend I met Gus Russell of my old Troop. He was limping along carrying a machine-gun tripod. He told me the shelling had been fierce and had played havoc with the trenches. His machine gun had been hit and put out of action. Old Doctor Holmes, the machine-gun Sergeant-Major, a fine fellow, had been killed when the gun was hit. In the midst of this havoc the Germans came over in masses, and by sheer weight of numbers had gained a footing in our trenches, which had been almost obliterated by the shelling.

'As the day wore on … bit by bit the details of the battle leaked down to us with the wounded men. We could scarcely credit these reports till at dusk the survivors hobbled back to the horse-lines … They looked bedraggled and weary to death as they marched in. Sinbad the Sailor (Reggie Wyndham) covered in mud, and a rifle slung over his shoulder like a Tommy, walked alone at the head of what remained of his troop. His Troop Sergeant, Cabby Dawes, had been wounded in the first bombardment, and as somebody tried to carry him back he had been hit again and killed. Sinbad and Cabby were kindred spirits and inseparable at all times. Neither had any thought for himself. Their horses were never short of forage, nor their men of rations. Better soldiers than those two and their Troop of scallywags and hard cases did not exist. Both A and D Squadrons had sustained losses, but C Squadron had, with the exception of Charlie Wright and six or seven men, been absolutely wiped out.'

Orders were issued to the Household Cavalry to withdraw to a second line and by 10.00 hours the British in the sector had retired in good order, except for the two squadrons on the left flank. The order did not reach these two squadrons and they suffered almost total extinction. About ten men got back, but all the remaining officers and other ranks were listed as missing, Lord Grosvenor and Lord Worsley (RHG) amongst them. Worsley was last seen directing his machine gun as shellfire exploded around him, the mound of enemy corpses before his position giving mute testimony to his team's action during the morning.

Officers leading the defence in the trenches by shouting orders, brandishing revolvers instead of rifles, and having metal 'pips' on their shoulders would have made attractive targets for advancing enemy soldiers. Lieutenant Reggie Wyndham retired from Zandvoorde with a rifle slung over his shoulder and it is likely that other officers, Lord Hugh included, also used rifles in this battle.

As the survivors made their way to the shelter of the woods at Klein Zillebeke Worsley's gun was heard chattering its defiance before an eerie silence embraced the Zandvoorde knoll.

In Jerry Murland's book, 'The Aristocrats Go To War', he sums up the battle:

'06.45 to 07.45 or 08.00 hours artillery bombardment at Zandvoorde where 7th Cavalry Brigade (1/ and 2/ Life Guards and Royal Horse Guards) are dug in on the forward slopes of the village. On their left flank are 1st Battalion Royal Welch Fusiliers. At 08.00 hours the German 39th Division attacks in force (and three Jäger Battalions) and two Squadrons of Life Guards and the Royal Horse Guards (Blues) machine-gun section are killed or captured. The Germans now in possession the entire Zandvoorde ridge.'

Lord Tweedmouth in RHG recalled the action:

'After an ominously quiet night the shelling begins all round our house and Brigade HQ. Jack Johnsons and heavy shrapnel, and hit several men. Corporal Turner came in wounded to say that C Squadron had been literally blown out of their trenches in the valley. Germans began to appear on the ridge, but not in large numbers. We retired slowly up the hill to Klein Zillebeke while our guns plastered the ridge. Worsley and MG Section missing also Hugh Grosvenor's Squadron and Alex Vandeleur's.'

By all accounts it appears the Zandvoorde ridge was in enemy hands sometime after 9.00 hours:

'By nine o'clock the Household Cavalry trenches had been literally blown to pieces ... Lord Hugh Grosvenor's Squadron of the 1st Life Guards 'C' Squadron the 2nd Life Guards, and Lord Worsley's machine-gun section of the Blues did not succeed in withdrawing with the rest of the brigade, and their fate is still a matter of uncertainty. It is probable, however, that, in the pandemonium which was reigning, the order to retire did not reach them, and that those who survived the bombardment awaited the infantry attack which followed, and fought it out to the absolute finish. It may well be that untold deeds of heroism remain yet to be recorded in connection with that morning's work.'

The bombardment with high explosive shells blew many of the trenches to bits. Those who survived would have been tired beyond belief – chilled to the bone having endured days and nights of lying in cold and wet stinking pits and their uniforms covered in oozing mud. Some soldiers would have been buried in their trenches, others suffering horrific wounds. Deafened and dazed they would have tried desperately to dig out their buried comrades and patch them up if they could. Eventually they would have become aware of masses of grey clad German soldiers steadily advancing forwards with bugles blaring and bands playing.

With the crack of small arms fire coming at them the defenders will have tried to clean off the mud and soil from their own rifles and start rapid fire into the seemingly endless hordes of attackers. Lord Worsley covered his precious machine gun with his own body to prevent it becoming fouled with mud and flying debris during the bombardment. First-hand accounts of assaults by Germans give nightmarish reports of German soldiers clambering over heaps of their own dead comrades and with grim determination they kept on coming. What they may have lacked in tactical training or battle experience they made up for in patriotic fervour and courage. Where Germans could exploit a gap in the front line, as at Kruiseeke, they would rush through to start firing along the length of the trench – enfilade fire. Otherwise they would move around the back of the position and attack the defenders from behind.

If Lord Hugh had not been incapacitated by shellfire all accounts of him would envisage him encouraging his men to do their duty and fight on steeped in the traditions of the chivalric code. Lord Hugh was not one to recoil in the face of the enemy. Inspired by lessons from history, and trained by the likes of Capper, he would have fought to the end.

As in other accounts of similar battles the defenders may have had to resort to search wounded or dead comrades for spare rounds. It would probably have been a dreadful and chaotic experience. It seems most likely that Lord Worsley's machine gun expended its ammunition. With continued artillery shells blowing trenches to bits the defenders would have continued to fire until they ran out of ammunition and their position was overrun. Hand-to-hand fighting, or close quarter battle, are euphemisms for being shot at point-blank range or meeting death at the point of a bayonet or from a rifle butt.

Stuart Menzies, the adjutant of 2/LG, described the battle as follows:

'On the 30th the Household Cavalry Regiments were in the front line … when the German attack was launched … practically nothing is known of what occurred as the two squadrons and machine guns of the Blues completely disappeared and only a few survivors were taken prisoner and on their return at the end of the war they were unable, I understand, to throw much light on the attack … the attack was made by German infantry after a very heavy preliminary bombardment. I can only conclude that the squadrons were cut off owing to their somewhat forward position and were ultimately all killed though it is remarkable that there should have been so few wounded taken prisoner. I fear that one must assume that the Germans behaved in an ultra–Hunlike manner and gave no quarter.'

The assumption Menzies makes about the lack of wounded defenders being taken prisoner by the Germans implies that they took no pity on the defenders and effectively gave them a *coupe de grace*, i.e. finished them off. There is no evidence of this so it remains merely speculation. Stuart Menzies (who later became head of MI6 and was the first 'M' of James Bond fame) gave a credible, albeit second hand, account.

The suspicion that the Germans acted in a dastardly way has been repeated by Paul Bessemer in his biography of Lord Worsley,

'The fact that no wounded or prisoners were taken started a rumour that Kaiser Wilhelm II (who was at von Fabeck's headquarters witnessing the battle) may have ordered any Household Cavalrymen left alive to be bayoneted and slaughtered where they lay. This may have been because the Royal Horse Guards and Life Guards were the favourite regiments and personal bodyguard of the Kaiser's cousin, King George V, and Wilhelm wanted it to be a massive blow to the morale and a huge personal insult to the King.'

No-one will ever know if this rumour was true. In any case, as there are no accounts of the Household Cavalrymen offering surrender, the suggestion that the Kaiser wanted the defenders annihilated is immaterial.

The 2/LG war diary reported:

'½ mile North West of Zandvoorde. C Squadron (less 1 Troop) would appear to have been surrounded and from the account of a single survivor of the squadron it is doubtful if any have escaped.

'The cavalry brigade was forced to retire slowly down the hill, keeping up a covering fire as it went. The retirement was effected in good order, but Lord Hugh Grosvenor's squadron of the 1st Life Guards, C Squadron of the 2nd Life Guards and Lord Worsley's machine-gun section of the Blues did not succeed in withdrawing with the rest of the brigade. An officer in the Royal Welch Fusiliers' trenches subsequently described the defence put up that day by the Household Cavalry as one of the finest feats of the war.'

The officer from the 1/RWF in the Kruiseke trenches would have had a good view of the defence put up by Lord Hugh's squadron. The observer would surely have commented if they had offered surrender. It seems likely therefore that Lord Hugh's soldiers stood their ground and fought to the last.

Most of Zandvoorde was captured by a composite force of Jäger battalions under the command of Major Petersen who commanded the 10th Jäger.

'By 11 am (in fact 10 am British time) the attackers had penetrated the British positions, but were stalled by … the bitter defence offered by the 1st Battalion of the Royal Welch Fusiliers.'

Eventually the enemy took complete control of the Zandvoorde ridge from where they proceeded to lay down enfilade fire on the right flank of the 7th Division, obliterating the 1/RWF which had been fighting off the massed infantry attacks themselves.

Once the position had been taken

'they rushed two batteries of artillery into the village and from the hill overlooking the Battalion began firing directly into the trenches. The Jägers working their way behind the Fusiliers, and from a farmhouse and ditch began shooting from only 30 yards. Although attacked on three sides by overwhelming odds, these hard professional soldiers with their four surviving officers fought on until near noon when, with ammunition running out and rifles jamming, they were finally overrun. The German records report every single one of the 54 Fusiliers captured was wounded.'

The 1/RWF mustered 86 survivors at roll call that evening from what had been a battalion of 1,100 men. These remnants were subsumed in the 2/Queen's Regiment with the only RWF officer left being the Quartermaster. The Germans 'consistently mistook the small numbers of defenders they confronted as representing merely an outpost line'. They usually overestimated the British strength. The attack on the Zandvoorde trenches was summarized by Lieutenant Colonel Ralph Bingham:

'The squadron belonging to the 1st Life Guards disappeared. It was surrounded and engulfed by the enemy. And surely this is the strangest thing of the Great War, for not one officer or man, not a button or a rifle, nothing of that squadron has ever been seen or heard of to this day. It was as though they had never been. No graves were ever discovered. No capture was ever reported. To-day I am glad to give these very gallant men a memory. They were commanded by one of the finest men I have ever known – Lord Hugh Grosvenor, and half-brother to the Duke of Westminster. Knowing them, I know they fought and died where they stood. Many strange things happened between 1914 and 1918, but to my mind there was nothing more dramatic, more mysterious then the disappearance "into the blue" of the Life Guards squadron.'

In a way Bingham was factually incorrect as there were a handful of survivors from the battlefield, but at the time he obviously believed they had been annihilated.

At the end of the First World War Haig recalled the battle:

'They were in narrow trenches on the forward slopes before us in full sight of the enemy. Their trenches were soon blown in and at 8 am after one and a quarter hours bombardment the whole of the 39th German Infantry Division and three battalions of Jaegers attacked their shattered position. The time had come to slip away and orders were issued for the retirement to the second line; but the greater part of two squadrons of Life Guards on the left and the Royal Horse Guards machine guns could not get away and were cut off and died to a man, except for a few wounded prisoners.'

Once the ridge had been taken the British cavalrymen vacated the area, leaving their dead comrades on a now German-occupied sector of a Flanders battlefield, but it had been a galling experience for the enemy who had been held back by so few British defenders. The British had not been able to halt the German move towards Ypres in this sector but the cost to the enemy had been heavy and valuable time was gained for the British Command.

The official German account read:

'Two whole British squadrons with their machine guns lay, dead and wounded completely annihilated in one meadow on the battlefield.'

The inference in mentioning 'machine guns' was that there were more than one although this was probably wrong as by all accounts there was only one. If the rest of the report is correct it would appear that the defenders had been blown to smithereens or left at the bottom of their trenches and simply buried where they lay.

In the afternoon the German 39th Infantry Division were ordered to launch an assault from Zandvoorde with the objective of capturing Zillebeke. However, 'the day had been too costly in casualties; too hard fought and the men were completely exhausted by the effort,' therefore, 'the troops were ordered to dig in where they were.'

The courage of the German troops at Ypres must be acknowledged. They advanced again and again in massed formations often in the face of artillery, machine-gun and rifle fire. Although some were well trained many had only the most rudimentary of basic military training. It is simply astonishing that these raw recruits attacked with such vigour. The German High Command repaid the compliment:

'The fact that neither the enemy's commanders nor their troops gave way under the strong pressure we put on them, but continued to fight the battle round Ypres, though their situation was most perilous, gives us an opportunity to acknowledge that these were men of real worth opposed to us who did their duty thoroughly.'

With Zandvoorde now in German hands the parlous state of the defence of the area was appreciated by Haig. The French military immediately responded to a request for assistance by sending a brigade of cavalry. The First Battle of Ypres was to grind on for several more weeks. On 31 October another massive German attack fell onto the Composite Regiment of Household Cavalry holding the line between Wytschaete and Messines. As Lieutenant Colonel Cook had been wounded and Major John Cavendish killed on 20 October 1914 command passed to Lord Hugh's brother-in-law Major Viscount Crichton.

In the face of near suicidal massed attacks by the German infantry the Composite Regiment could hold on no longer and Major Crichton ordered a withdrawal of his regiment as the Lincoln Regiment came to reinforce the line. In this action Major Crichton was killed and became the only Household Cavalryman to have a marked grave in the Zandvoorde Cemetery. On the following day the Composite Regiment mustered 30 soldiers from 1/LG, 3 from 2/LG and 30 from RHG. The regiment was disbanded and the survivors returned to their parent units on 11 November.

The British press reported:

'Severe fighting continues with little intermission along the Allies' line, especially towards the north. The German resistance is stubborn, and fierce counter attacks are made by them frequently; nevertheless the British are still gaining ground. Yesterday the Germans attempted violent counter attacks on the French and British army corps who were advancing to the north-east and east of Ypres.'

From a German source,

'Our attacks to the south of Nieuport and east of Ypres are being successfully continued. Eight machine guns and 200 British soldiers have been captured.'

It is revealing that German assaults are reported by the British as 'counter-attacks' as if these are in response to British attacks. Likewise German 'stubborn resistance' is actually veiled speech representing German advances.

The actions on 30 October 1914 cost the Allies hundreds of casualties in terms of killed, wounded, missing and prisoners. Amazingly in Britain this was reduced to a mere few column inches in the national newspapers. Either the press were not aware of the facts or, if they were, they were restricted in what they could print. It is interesting to compare and contrast journalism then and now. Everyone today in the social media age is their own citizen-journalist. It would be inconceivable that such meagre coverage would be given to such catastrophic loss of life today.

As the First Battle of Ypres raged on into November the defence of Zandvoorde ridge with the loss of over one hundred soldiers from the Household Cavalry was dwarfed by similar actions around the Ypres salient. Indeed the following two days were even more intense and desperate as the Allied forces fought for their survival.

Captain Lord Hugh William Grosvenor was first buried at Zandvoorde, but his grave was lost in later shelling. It was common knowledge that the Germans were familiar with the names of many English notables who served in the Guards and the Household Cavalry. It was likely that they knew Lord Grosvenor was in the trenches at Zandvoorde and that he was related to the Duke of Westminster. Likewise, it is probable that they knew that Lieutenant the Honourable Gerald Ward of the same Regiment was also in the Zandvoorde trenches and a brother of the Earl of Dudley.

In the doomed Royal Welch Fusilier trenches was the heir to the Oulton estate, Little Budworth in Cheshire. Captain Rowland le Belward Egerton was only 19 years old and served in the RWF; by coincidence he also died on 30 October 1914 at Zandvoorde in the Kruiseke trenches near where the Zantvoorde British Cemetery now lies. Rowland has no known grave and his name is engraved on the Ploegsteert Memorial. He was one of two sons of Sir Philip Brian Grey-Egerton who lived at Oulton Park Hall (now a motor racing circuit).

Rowland's twin brother Philip served as a Captain in 19th Hussars. It appears he never got over the death of Rowland. Whilst recuperating at Oulton Park Hall, suffering from post-traumatic stress, and against the wishes of his father, Philip managed to rejoin his regiment. Tragically the telegram to cancel Philip's return to his regiment arrived at Oulton Park Hall just after he had set off for Crewe railway station. Philip died on 8 October 1918 at Busigny in France only a few days before the Armistice. All gave some; some gave all.

The battle raged on and the Germans renewed their attack on Gheluvelt with their 54th Reserve Division and their 30th Division. This attack was halted. The *Daily Graphic* reported on 2 November:

> 'The Germans have continued their violent attacks in the whole of the northern region. To the east and south of Ypres all these attacks have been repulsed and we have even made slight progress to the north of Ypres and perceptible progress to the east of that locality.'

In the absence of hard facts it seems that the press were willing to put a positive gloss on the situation. The art of 'spin' is by no means a modern media phenomenon.

In 1940 the Battle of Britain was a pivotal moment. By failing to defeat the Royal Air Force Hitler's planned invasion of Great Britain was over. In retrospect the First Battle of Ypres was also such a pivotal moment. It may not have been patently obvious to anyone at the time but, by not taking Ypres that day, the Germans would not be able to win the war. They had played their hand and lost; the Allied line would hold and it would take four years of fighting before an armistice was agreed. As Morgan Crofton wrote:
'The German strategists, once their carefully elaborate scheme for crushing France was foiled, showed loss of military judgment and indecision.'

For the Germans therefore the war was effectively over. The tragedy is that it took the lives of millions of men and women over the following years to realize it.

Chapter 12

The Aftermath

The quality of the cavalrymen in the First Battle of Ypres was praised by historian Simon Robbins as he described an action the day after Lord Hugh was killed at Zandvoorde:

> '31 October was a day of crisis with the Cavalry Corps being forced off the Messines Ridge after heavy fighting. The Cavalry Corps held on and "in holding at bay so greatly superior a mass of enemy infantry, performed a feat of defence unrivalled in history by any other cavalry".'

This was to be the last hurrah of the cavalry and indeed of the old regular army prior to the stalemate on the Western Front and the subsequent dominance of trench warfare.

> 'Nothing can ever surpass, as a story of simple, sublime pluck, the history of the first three months of Britain's participation in the First World War.'

On 31 October 1914 Kaiser Wilhelm II arrived at Courtrai Belgium to celebrate what was assumed would be a triumphant ride through the gates of Ypres. The Old Contemptibles caused a re-scheduling in the Kaiser's appointment diary and he was never to enter Ypres. By mid-November the initial phase of the First World War was concluded. For Lord Hugh and thousands of others on both sides their war was already over, but it would drag on for four more bloody years until the Armistice of 11 November 1918.

The death of Lord Hugh and countless other titled soldiers often caused massive repercussions to the aristocracy. Sometimes modest estates ceased to exist following two lots of death duties in quick succession after the death of the incumbent and an heir. Nearly 30,000 estates were sold in the first decade after the First World War. 'Most of these were disposed of by fathers who no longer had sons to inherit.' Also, with so many of the landed gentry being killed (or in khaki) at the time of the 1918 General Election it was businessmen who now filled the positions of political leadership in Great Britain. It was quite literally the end of an era. The Foreign Secretary, Sir Edward Grey, is quoted as saying on the eve of the war: 'The lamps are going out all over Europe, we shall not see them lit again in our life-time.'

The publication of Debrett's Peerage and Baronetage in 1915 was severely delayed because 'so many heirs to great lands and titles had been killed … The death toll in the last months of 1914 changed the social landscape of Britain forever.'

Whether Lord Hugh's soldiers were inspired by the 'big picture' of their strategic position, or fought it out in a valiant attempt to protect the flanks of their comrades in the Royal Welch Fusiliers will remain unanswered questions. What is unquestionable is that the defenders fought to the last man. The qualities of the British officer were highlighted by Simon Robbins as,

'resilience, tenacity, an ability to learn, and a growing expertise, which would eventually pull the British Army through the war and make victory possible.'

Although Lord Hugh's resting place is unknown, his comrade Lord Worsley's body was located by a German officer:

'Just before dusk … Oberleutnant Freiherr von Prankh went to inspect the captured trenches, and he made for the place where … Worsley and his section had kept firing their single gun … He stepped gingerly into the shallow trench, for it was full of dead men. The machine gun had tumbled backwards on top of the gunners' bodies and the arm of the dead officer was trapped beneath the barrel. Von Prankh bent down to search the body and was astonished by what he found. His adversary of the morning was his own exact counterpart. Von Prankh was a cavalryman and a machine-gun officer and a member of the German nobility.'

The area was strewn with German and British dead and the latter were likely to be buried in mass graves. Oberleutnant Freiheer Von Prankh ordered one of his Lieutenants to bury Lord Worsley which he did. He also made a sketch map of Worsley's grave and noted that 'countless grey-clad corpses of German dead lay in drifts.' The map, giving the position of Lord Worsley's grave, was passed to the family through diplomatic channels and was later identified.

In December 1918, armed with a copy of Von Prankh's map by Lady Yarborough (Lord Worsley's mother), Colonel A. W. James MC located Lord Worsley's original grave. He was assisted by a former cavalryman from the 10th Hussars who fought at Zandvoorde. The marker post for the grave was 'standing on what had once been a shell-hole, now a tangle of rough, overgrown vegetation.'

In January of the following year Colonel James returned to the grave site with Lord Worsley's brother, Sackville Pelham. After replacing the original wooden cross with a more permanent one the original, plus an osier (willow) cutting, were brought home. Willows from the cutting now grow at Herstmonceux Castle (Colonel James' home), Brocklesby Estate (Lord Worsley's home) and Combermere Barracks, Windsor. The original grave marker was installed along with Lord Worsley's sword in Brocklesby Church Lincolnshire. The plot of land was bought by Lady Worsley and in September 1921 Lord Worsley's body was exhumed and reburied in Military Extension No 291 of the Ypres Town Cemetery.

Back in Lord Worsley's parish church, All Saints at Brocklesby Lincolnshire, a monument in his honour was inscribed:

'Brave, courteous, loving and beloved,
he died the noblest death a man may die
fighting for God and right and liberty
and such a death is immortality.'

On 19 December 1914 Cox's Shipping Agency of Charing Cross confirmed that they had forwarded Lord Hugh's personal effects: 'Field Kit no 2595, 2596 and 3188' to Lady Hugh Grosvenor at Southwick Crescent, Hyde Park.

On 25 January 1916 the Army Council wrote to Lady Hugh Grosvenor regretting that they had no reports concerning Lord Hugh and unless further

The telegram everyone dreaded. On 4 November 1914 this War Office telegram was delivered to Lady Mabel Grosvenor stating,

'Regret to inform you that Captain Lord Hugh Grosvenor is reported missing 25 – 31 October. This does not necessarily mean he is killed or wounded.' (*Private Collection*)

news had reached her they 'will regretfully be constrained to conclude that he died'. Her steadfast response was that she refused to give up hope that her husband could be alive and accordingly, without some definite proof of his death, that 'no presumption of Lord Hugh Grosvenor's death will be published.'

Initially Lady Hugh Grosvenor (Mabel Florence Mary Crichton, 2nd daughter of the 4th Earl of Erne) believed that her husband had survived the battle. The *Daily Graphic* in 1916 reported:

'There is good reason for believing that the Earl of Erne and his brother-in-law, Lord Hugh Grosvenor, are in captivity on a German island, where they are very specially guarded. They have been missing from the early days of the war, and no direct news of either has been received from that day to this. The Countess of Erne has a firm conviction that

her husband is alive, and this is shared by her mother, the Dowager
Countess of Erne whose daughter, Lady Hugh Grosvenor, is equally
sanguine as to Lord Hugh Grosvenor being alive.'

Although the story seems far-fetched it represented the last hope for a
distressed family. Lord Hugh was reported as missing and there were no
reports that he was wounded or killed. The press reports on 31 October 1914
state from German sources that '200 British soldiers have been captured.'
Therefore Lady Grosvenor could have clung to the notion that her husband
had been one of those captured. From Lady Grosvenor's perspective no
body had been identified; prisoners had been allegedly taken and there
was the possibility (however remote) that her husband was being held
incommunicado. It is certainly true that British prisoners of war (POW)
were held on German islands in the Baltic Sea during the First World
War. There is nothing in The *Daily Graphic* report giving any evidence to
substantiate notion that the Earl of Erne (actually Major, brevet Lieutenant
Colonel, Viscount Henry William Crichton DSO MVO of the Royal Horse
Guards) and Lord Hugh Grosvenor were prisoners. As Viscount Crichton
was killed in action on 31 October 1914 and buried at the Zantvoorde *(sic)*
British Cemetery the belief that he was alive and being held as a POW was
unlikely. The Army Council again wrote to Lady Hugh Grosvenor on 18
March 1919 concluding that Lord Hugh was probably dead. On 18 August
1919, at the request of the family solicitors (Boodle, Hatfield and Company),
the Army Council issued a letter in lieu of a death certificate confirming that
they had no doubt that Lord Hugh died either in 'France or Belgium on, or
after, 30 October 1914'. On 13 May 1920 Ed Brassey and his wife Maggs
visited Zandvoorde ridge and took photographs of the area including Lord
Worsley's grave marker cross.

In her letter to Lady Hugh Grosvenor Maggs wrote:

'It's marvellous the way the flowers have grown and one feels the
hideousness of it is gently veiled from one and though one sees the
broken ground, the shell holes full of water still there are always flowers
and masses of broom, great patches of yellow. The absolute wreckage
of towns and villages is quite inconceivable.'

The following photographs were taken in May 1920 around Zandvoorde.

'Grave looking north towards Zandtvoorde.' The grave is of Lord Worsley before his body was reburied in Ypres. (*Private Collection*)

'Looking left grave in foreground.' The water-logged depression on the left could have been the after effect of shelling. (*Private Collection*)

'Looking east. Mound nr 2nd LG position.' The unsuitability of the ground for trench digging is apparent by the water logged shell holes. (*Private Collection*)

'Looking south from ridge.' (*Private Collection*)

Taken from mound looking across road running from Zandvoorde to Tenbrielen.'
(*Private Collection*)

The view from the Zandvoorde ridge today looking East. (*Wayne Evans*)

As well as the tragedy of losing her husband and bringing up her two sons Lady Hugh Grosvenor threw herself into supporting the war effort by organizing a chain of YMCA canteens for munitions workers. For this endeavour she was awarded an MBE in 1919.

Eventually Mabel had to accept the sad fact that her husband, Lord Hugh, was dead and she was now a widow. In 1920 she married Robert Hamilton-Stubber, a former 1/LG officer, and good friend of Lord Hugh. A son (John Henry) was born and she died in 1944.

Her first two sons both became Dukes of Westminster, Gerald Hugh Grosvenor the 4th Duke of Westminster 1963 to 1967 and Robert George Grosvenor the 5th Duke of Westminster from 1967 to 1979.

Conclusion

The time gained by Lord Hugh and his men allowed the allied high command to reinforce and re-establish a new front line. Morgan Crofton commented: 'If the 3rd Cavalry Division and the 7th Infantry Division had not held the gap round Ypres … whilst our troops were coming up from Soissons, the Germans would have occupied Calais, and all of the French coast which is nearest England. The British Army has covered itself with the greatest glory.'

The First Battle of Ypres was the virtual death of the pre-war British regular army:

'Britain was cruelly hit. Her small and precious regular army was fast melting away and she had nothing behind it but good raw material!'

The battle also saw the apotheosis of British regular soldiers, but also their end. Many of the 'Old Contemptibles' were dead and those remaining were soon to be distributed among 1,000 new battalions. It was the end of the old army, and an older and freer mode of war. For now a huge, cumbrous mechanism had cast a blight of paralysis on human endeavour. The fronts had been stricken by their vastness into stagnation. Trenches stretched from Switzerland to the North Sea.

If the battle was the death knell of the regular army it also marked the demise of the traditional cavalryman.

The cavalryman in 1914 could trace his military lineage back to the days of knights in armour. Lord Hugh saw the end of this dynasty. As Major the Hon J. J. Astor MP (late 1/LG) stated:

'The day may not be distant when some trumpeter will sound the last dismount. Thereafter the fighting man will rely only upon the instruments which men have fashioned – and so farewell to much of chivalry.'

Undoubtedly the cavalry had saved the BEF in its retreat from Mons:

'The future of the cavalry … is at present uncertain. Nobody, however, can deny that this arm has rendered the most important services during this war. The retreat from Mons … was only rendered possible because of the screen of cavalry which enveloped the rear of the retreating II Corps.'

According to Hubert Gough: 'The opposing forces settled down to trench warfare in a spirit of earnest resignation.' This new line was to hold until the following year when poison gas preceded a German offensive.

Eventually the Battle of Amiens in August 1918 was the start of the Hundred Days Offensive where, with meticulous planning and the coordinated use of artillery, machine guns, tanks, aircraft and skill-at-arms, the Allies pushed the Germans back through their defensive Hindenburg Line and defeated them convincingly.

Crippled by years of the Royal Navy's blockade on Germany; wracked by civil unrest and mutinies at home; and being defeated in the field by the Allies, led by Britain, the Imperial German Army was forced to ask for an Armistice or face total collapse. A hollow victory was won.

What happened to Lord Hugh and the other defenders of Zandvoorde is unknown. One conclusion is that everyone in the unit who were not killed by the bombardment fought to the death without offering surrender. In those days the concept of throwing in the towel was alien, especially to an army led by an officer corps predominantly educated at public school.

It seems incredible that the soldiers did not simply flee the battlefield. Withdrawal from harm's way is simply the human survival instinct functioning correctly after all.

'What is remarkable is that with the exception of two individuals in the whole army during the period October-November there were no cases of cowardice or desertion or quitting a post under fire.'

Lord Hugh was both an observer, and regrettably a victim, of a watershed in military history. The end of the horse mounted warrior (the knight) coincided with the advent of the industrialization of conflict with mechanized war-machines, artillery, machine guns, aircraft and armoured vehicles. All these were mentioned in Lord Hugh's letters home.

The fortunes of war deprived him of a marked grave. It is very probable that he lies with his fellow officers and soldiers of his Squadron on the little ridge just east of the peaceful village of Zandvoorde overlooking the historic old town of Ypres. Lord Hugh set standards in stoicism, duty, service and ultimately noble sacrifice. History records that he and nearly a million of his countrymen lost their lives in the Great War; that this war was not the 'war to end all wars' was a tragedy. As each Remembrance Sunday approaches it is important to reflect on the sacrifices servicemen and servicewomen have made for our freedom today and resolve to learn the lessons from the past. The soldiers had done everything their King and Empire could ask of them. They fought to protect our country and their comrades from defeat. Lord Hugh was the embodiment of the steadfast British spirit.

A survivor of Ypres commented:

'The register of killed and wounded … tells, in the simplest terms, a tale of death and mutilation faced and found at the call of duty. Let us leave it at that.'

British Army at Ypres 1914

The major elements of the British forces which were involved in The First Battle of Ypres consisted of the remnants of the BEF, i.e. the Cavalry Corps, I Corps and II Corps, which were joined in August by III Corps and in October by IV Corps.

General Headquarters – Commander-in-Chief Field Marshal Sir John French
Cavalry Corps – General Officer Commanding Lieutenant General Edmund Allenby
1st Cavalry Division – General Officer Commanding Major General Henry de Beauvior de Lisle
1st Cavalry Brigade – General Officer Commanding Brigadier General C. J. Briggs
2nd Dragoon Guards
5th Dragoon Guards
11th Hussars
2nd Cavalry Brigade
4th Dragoon Guards
9th Lancers
18th Hussars

2nd Cavalry Division – General Officer Commanding Major General Herbert Gough
3rd Cavalry Brigade
4th Hussars
5th Lancers
16th Lancers
4th Cavalry Brigade – General Officer Commanding Brigadier General C. E. Bingham

Composite Regiment of Household Cavalry

6th Dragoon Guards

3rd Hussars

5th Cavalry Brigade – General Officer Commanding Brigadier General Sir Philip Chetwode

2nd Dragoons

12th Lancers

20th Hussars

I Corps – General Officer Commanding Lieutenant General Sir Douglas Haig

1st Division – General Officer Commanding Major General Samuel Lomax

1st (Guards) Brigade – General Officer Commanding Brigadier General Ivor Maxse

1st Coldstream Guards

1st Scots Guards

1st Black Watch (Royal Highlanders)

1st Cameron Highlanders

2nd Brigade – General Officer Commanding Brigadier General Edward Bulfin

2nd Royal Sussex Regiment

1st Loyal North Lancashire Regiment

1st Northamptonshire Regiment

2nd King's Royal Rifle Corps

3rd Brigade – General Officer Commanding Brigadier General Herman Landon

1st Queen's (Royal West Surrey Regiment)

1st South Wales Borderers

1st Gloucestershire Regiment

2nd Welch Regiment

2nd Division – General Officer Commanding Major General Charles Monro

4th (Guards) Brigade – General Officer Commanding Brigadier General R. Scott-Kerr

2nd Grenadier Guards

2nd Coldstream Guards

3rd Coldstream Guards

1st Irish Guards

5th Brigade – General Officer Commanding Brigadier General R. C. B. Haking

2nd Worcestershire Regiment

2nd Oxfordshire and Buckinghamshire Light Infantry

2nd Highland Light Infantry

2nd Connaught Rangers

6th Brigade – General Officer Commanding Brigadier General R. H. Davies

1st King's (Liverpool) Regiment

2nd South Staffordshire Regiment

1st Princess Charlotte of Wales's Own (Royal Berkshire) Regiment

1st King's Royal Rifle Corps

II Corps – General Officer Commanding General Sir Horace Smith-Dorrien

3rd Division – General Officer Commanding Major General Hurbert Hamilton

7th Brigade – General Officer Commanding Brigadier General F. W. N. McCracken

3rd Worcestershire Regiment

2nd Prince of Wales's Volunteers (South Lancashire) Regiment

1st Duke of Edinburgh's (Wiltshire Regiment)

2nd Royal Irish Rifles

8th Brigade – General Officer Commanding Brigadier General B. J. C. Doran

2nd Royal Scots (Lothian Regiment)

2nd Royal Irish

4th The Duke of Cambridge's Own (Middlesex Regiment)

1st Devonshire Regiment

9th Brigade – General Officer Commanding Brigadier General F. C. Shaw

1st Northumberland Fusiliers

4th Royal Fusiliers (City of London Regiment)

1st Lincolnshire Regiment

1st Royal Scots Fusiliers

5th Division – General Officer Commanding Major General Sir Charles Fergusson

13th Brigade – General Officer Commanding Brigadier General G. J. Cuthbert

2nd King's Own Scottish Borderers

2nd Duke of Wellington's Regiment (West Riding Regiment)

1st The Queen's Own (Royal West Kent Regiment)

2nd King's Own Yorkshire Light Infantry

14th Brigade – General Officer Commanding Brigadier General S. P. Rolt

2nd Suffolk Regiment

1st East Surrey Regiment

1st Duke of Cornwall's Light Infantry

2nd Manchester Regiment

15th Brigade – General Officer Commanding Brigadier General Count Gleichen

1st Norfolk Regiment

1st Bedfordshire Regiment

1st Cheshire Regiment

1st Dorsetshire Regiment

III Corps – General Officer Commanding Major General William Pulteney

4th Division – General Officer Commanding Major General Thomas Snow

10th Brigade – General Officer Commanding Brigadier General J. A. L. Haldane

1st Royal Warwickshire Regiment

2nd Seaforth Highlanders

1st Royal Irish Fusiliers

2nd Royal Dublin Fusiliers

11th Brigade – General Officer Commanding Brigadier General A. G. Hunter-Weston

1st Somerset Light Infantry

1st East Lancashire Regiment

1st Hampshire Regiment

1st Rifle Brigade

12th Brigade – General Officer Commanding Brigadier General H. F. M. Wilson

1st Royal Lancaster Regiment

2nd Lancashire Fusiliers

2nd Royal Inniskilling Fusiliers

2nd Essex Regiment

6th Division – General Officer Commanding Major General J. L. Keir

16th Brigade – General Officer Commanding Brigadier General E. C. Ingouville-Williams

1st The Buffs (East Kent Regiment)

1st Leicestershire Regiment

1st Shropshire Light Infantry

2nd York and Lancaster Regiment

17th Brigade – General Officer Commanding Brigadier General W. R. B. Doran

1st Royal Fusiliers

1st Prince of Wales's (North Staffordshire Regiment)

2nd Prince of Wales's Leinster Regiment

3rd Rifle Brigade

18th Brigade – General Officer Commanding Brigadier General W. N. Congreve VC

1st The Prince of Wales's Own (West Yorkshire Regiment)

1st East Yorkshire Regiment

2nd Sherwood Foresters (Nottinghamshire & Derbyshire Regiment)

2nd Durham Light Infantry

IV Corps – General Officer Commanding Lieutenant General Sir Henry Rawlinson

7th Division – General Officer Commanding Major General Thompson Capper

20th Brigade – General Officer Commanding Brigadier General Ruggles-Brise

1st Grenadier Guards

2nd Scots Guards

2nd Border Regiment

2nd Gordon Highlanders

21st Brigade – General Officer Commanding Brigadier General H. E. Watts

2nd Bedfordshire Regiment

2nd Green Howards

2nd Royal Scots Fusiliers

2nd Wiltshire Regiment

22nd Brigade – General Officer Commanding Brigadier General S. T. B. Lawford

2nd Queen's (Royal West Surrey Regiment)

2nd Royal Warwickshire Regiment

1st Royal Welch Fusiliers

1st South Staffordshire Regiment

3rd Cavalry Division – General Officer Commanding Major General J. H. G. Byng

6th Cavalry Brigade – General Officer Commanding Brigadier General E. Makins

3rd Dragoon Guards

1st Royal Dragoons

10th Hussars

7th Cavalry Brigade – General Officer Commanding Brigadier General C. T. Kavanagh

1st Life Guards

2nd Life Guards

Royal Horse Guards (Blues)

Indian Expeditionary Force

Line of Communication Defence independent brigade 19th Brigade – General Officer Commanding Major General L. G. Drummond

2nd Royal Welch Fusiliers

1st Cameronians

1st Middlesex

2nd Argyll and Sutherland Highlanders

Royal Flying Corps – General Officer Commanding Brigadier General Sir David Henderson

2nd Aeroplane Squadron

3rd Aeroplane Squadron

4th Aeroplane Squadron

5th Aeroplane Squadron

6th Aeroplane Squadron

Analysis

The loss of an entire unit is a mystery and many questions are still left unanswered.

Why are there no first-hand accounts of the fighting?
The main reason that no first-hand accounts from any soldier from Lord Hugh's squadron exist is probably because none of them withdrew. An unconfirmed report that a handful of soldiers were taken prisoner by the Germans, but could not give an account of the battle after the war, seems unlikely. There are no reports that any of C Squadron tried to retire. This could be for many reasons. Two factors which contribute to a soldier standing and fighting rather than retreating; one is the enduring stoic character of the British 'Tommy'; the other is the influence of an effective leader.

Was there was some coordinated defence?
There were reports of a 'roar of rifle and machine-gun fire' coming from the Zandvoorde fighting trench. It is likely that some leaders were still actively leading the defence and encouraging the troops. Lord Worsley was not far from Lord Hugh. The last time Lord Worsley was seen alive he was directing the fire of his machine guns. If Lord Hugh was still alive after the bombardment it is likely that he would be doing the same – leading by example and directing the defence of his trenches.

Why did no message get through to C Squadron to withdraw?
Two soldiers had been dispatched to give the order to Lord Hugh to retire, both these 'runners' had been killed trying to deliver the message. There was obviously no alternative means of communication. Field telephones were used in the First World War but the land lines were vulnerable to artillery fire.

Communications became a major part of conducting warfare. In January 1915 Morgan Crofton wrote,

'Went over the signalling equipment which we shall want in the trenches, as we are going to take good care that we are not left, as we were in November, without any communications between the front and rear trenches.'

Why did they not withdraw anyway?
The exposed position of the trenches and the hail of artillery and small arms fire meant that even if Lord Hugh's squadron had tried to withdraw they would probably have been annihilated.

'In the chaos of hand-to-hand fighting and the general pandemonium of combat, the order to retire did not reach all the cavalry positions … the machine-gun section of the Blues and one Squadron from each Regiment of 1/ and 2/ Life Guards held their positions and fought to the last man.'

The chaos of battle is termed the 'fog of war'. Even in the immediate aftermath of 30 October 1914 confusion reigned regarding what had happened to Lord Hugh and his squadron. An example of this is the report noted earlier of an officer of the Life Guards originally reported as missing who reappeared a few weeks later in a London military hospital with no recollection of the battle or how he arrived back in England.

Why did the defenders not surrender?
If Lord Hugh survived the bombardment he could possibly have ordered his soldiers to surrender. An Old Etonian of Lord Hugh's vintage would have been steeped in loyalty to his team and would never have wanted to let his comrades down. Maybe he would have been inspired by the recent actions at Mons, Elouges, La Cateau, Etreux, Villers-Cottrets, Néry and especially Gheluvelt.

Had the defenders offered surrender at an early stage in the battle when the infantry attack started it is possible that the German forces would have been a viable fighting force when they took the Zandvoorde ridge and had the strength to use the high ground as a springboard to continue their advance westwards. The survival of the British forces may have been the result of the tenacity of Lord Hugh's squadron in defending the indefensible position to the last.

In March 1918 the Imperial German Army, reinforced by troops redeployed from fighting the Russians in the East, launched a final great offensive against the French and British to win the war before American manpower and resources tipped the balance in the Allies favour. Reflecting on the huge number of British soldiers, mainly conscripts, who surrendered during this attack Martin Middlebrook commented:

> 'It would be commonly accepted that the duty of a soldier in action is to offer resistance to an enemy as long as he has a weapon and ammunition to do so and has not been incapacitated by a serious wound … A soldier who fights to the death, inflicting as much loss as possible on the enemy in doing so, is performing his ultimate duty. A soldier who surrenders while still in possession of a weapon, ammunition and while remaining unwounded, is of no further use to his country in time of war. These rules, so rarely written out or explicitly stated, are the harsh facts of a soldier's life… throughout this book these "conditions of service" were not fulfilled by thousands of men on 21st March 1918.'

By 1918 the British Army was predominantly made up of conscripts and, although there were some notable actions, such as the dogged defence of Manchester Hill outside Saint Quentin by Lieutenant Colonel Wilfrith Elstob VC whose Manchester Pals fought to the end, there were many incidents where more pragmatic leaders ordered surrender once their position was hopelessly untenable. This attitude was uncommon amongst the officer corps in 1914. It was simply not in their nature to give in.

Did the defenders try and surrender?
It is possible that an offer of surrender by the defenders was not accepted by the attackers. It would be understandable that the advancing infantry would not be in the mood to be magnanimous and take prisoners if their ranks

had been decimated by the fire from the defenders. It is much more likely, however, that no quarter was asked or given.

Why did the Germans not continue their advance?
Standard military tactics during the war would be to set an objective beyond the first line of trenches. The attackers would take the first line trench and push on to the second, or reserve, line trenches. It is unusual therefore that the Germans stopped at the ridge and did not carry on and open the way to Ypres. The defenders of the trenches had inflicted such damage that any further advance was impractical. It is reported that the corpses of the enemy dead lay in heaps before the Zandvoorde trenches. If this was the case the sacrifice that the defenders made in staying put and fighting to the last man saved the day, and may have even saved the rest of the British troops from a headlong retreat back to Ypres. In fact so real were the concerns that the Germans would break through in the Ypres area that the French High Command ordered the construction of a fortified zone around the Channel ports to begin on 28 October 1914.

What happened to Lord Hugh and his men?
Sadly only 20 per cent of those soldiers who died in the Salient have known graves. Most, including Lord Hugh and his squadron, are listed on the Menin Gate in Ypres as missing. Every evening the last post is sounded at the Menin Gate in tribute to the sacrifice of the soldiers who passed along the road and never returned. The inscription on the gate '*Dulce et Decorum est Pro Patria Mori*' (It is right and fitting to die for one's country) would have been well known to Lord Hugh and his classmates educated in Latin. Reading Lord Hugh's letters, however, he was obviously living life to the full, loved his wife and children dearly and relished the prospect of returning home when his duty had been done. It was not in his manner to give his life, or that of his soldiers, cheaply or capriciously.

When Lord Worsley's body was found after the battle it was by a massive shell hole created by a German howitzer. It is speculation, but quite possible, that the same shell could have accounted for Lord Hugh. If so death would probably have been instantaneous.

Why was Lord Hugh not decorated for bravery?
Although Lord Hugh was Mentioned in Dispatches in the London Gazette 17 February 1915 he was not awarded a medal for his valiant defence of the Zandvoorde ridge. To be awarded a gallantry medal the action must be witnessed by a commissioned officer. No-one was left to give any such account. According to Captain Lord Ernest Hamilton:

'V.C.s it is true were won; but for every one given a hundred were earned. Military honours are the fruit of recommendation; but when Generals, Colonels, Company Officers and Sergeants are no more, the deed must be its own record; there is none left to recommend.'

On 12 November 1914 Lieutenant Jack Dimmer of the 2nd King's Royal Rifle Corps manned a machine gun a few miles away from Zandvoorde at Klein Zillebeke and was awarded the last Victoria Cross during the First Battle of Ypres. He wrote,

'My face is splattered with pieces of my own gun and pieces of shell, and I have a bullet in my face and four holes in my right shoulder. It made rather a nasty mess of me.'

Dimmer was later killed in action on 21 March 1918 leading his soldiers. This action is very similar to that performed by Lord Worsley and had the courageous efforts of Lord Hugh and his soldiers been witnessed gallantry awards would have been justified.

Why were the bodies never found?
The ridge was much contested over the following days/weeks and it would have been an imperative for the Germans in their newly acquired position to bury the dead as quickly as possible. These battlefield burials were common place in the First World War as even now the rich soil of France and Belgium gives up its dead.

Looking at the fields around Zandvoorde today one is tempted to think that an excavation along the trench line could unearth the remains of Lord Hugh's Squadron – like the Chinese Terracotta Army – just waiting to be uncovered. It is only by researching eye witness accounts of similar battlefields that one can appreciate the futility of such an enterprise.

In Ernst Jünger's account of fighting for the German Army at Guillemont on the Somme one can almost image the chaos of a First World War battlefield:

'The defile proved to be little more than a series of enormous craters full of pieces of uniform, weapons and dead bodies; the country around, so far as the eye could see, had been completely ploughed by heavy shells. Not a single blade of grass showed itself. The churned up field was gruesome. In among the living defenders lay the dead. When we dug foxholes, we realized that they were stacked in layers. One company after another, pressed together in the drumfire, had been mown down, then the bodies had been buried under showers of earth sent up by shells, and then the relief company had taken their predecessors' place. And now it was our turn.'

The scene on Zandvoorde ridge would have been truly awful and any hope of finding the resting place of Lord Hugh well-nigh impossible. Oberleutnant Freiherr van Prankh's account of inspecting the trenches at the end of the battle has already been mentioned. The ridge stayed in enemy hands until 1918 and was repeatedly shelled, probably disturbing the remains of the dead over and over again.

What lessons were learnt about trench positioning?
Several times observers have mentioned the perilous nature of the trenches at Zandvoorde. As the war progressed the positioning of fire trenches became a subject requiring meticulous consideration which addressed the questions of 'securing good observation for ourselves and denying it to the enemy, cohesion in defence by mutual support of adjoining works.'

Unless the ground is almost absolutely flat, the most important question in siting trenches is whether to occupy the tops of the hills, establishing the front line trenches on either the crest or the forward slope, or to withdraw the main front line to the reverse slope. The chief argument advanced in favour of this latter position is that it affords greater security against hostile artillery fire.

Front line trenches on the ... forward slope are certainly exposed to view and therefore to bombardment ... the disadvantage can be diminished by adequate provision of material protection for the garrison.

From the pamphlet *Notes from the Front* in 1914:

'The enemy's artillery is numerous, powerful and efficient, and our infantry has suffered much from its fire. The German infantry, on the other hand, is inferior to our own in developing fire effect. A short field of fire (500 yards or even less) has been found sufficient to check a German infantry attack. Tactically, therefore, in occupying ground for defence, every effort should be made to combine the fire of our own guns and rifles against the enemy's infantry, while denying the enemy the use of his artillery by the siting of trenches in positions which it is intended to hold on to, behind rather than on the crest line or forward slopes!'

So a reverse slope position may have been safer for the defenders. If they had to have a forward slope position then overhead bomb-proof protection would be needed. In the First Battle of Ypres there were very few entrenching tools to hand let along proper trench materiel. Also the Flanders ground was too soft and turned too readily to mud to make deep trenches and dugouts.

What lessons were learnt about machine-gun positioning?
If the trenches were not well sited could Lord Worsley's machine guns be better placed? When considering machine-gun emplacements they should receive

'very special attention and care. They should be arranged so as to bring a cross fire to bear in front of the trenches which they protect. In this way their power is more fully developed and also concealment is easier ... machine-gun emplacements should be constructed so as to be as inconspicuous as possible. Both sides are constantly on the lookout to try and locate the enemy's machine-gun emplacements and any suspected spot is certain to be made the target for bombardment.'

Concealing the location of a machine-gun was of the utmost importance as Lord Worsley's father (Lord Yarbourough) wrote,

'He took the keenest interest in his gun and was so proud of it, and his one idea appeared to be to make his M/G section as perfect as possible. He talked and thought so much of the new work on which he was employed and told his parents with pride how, on occasion of a field-day at Aldershot, he had hidden his gun (specially painted to avoid detection) and the men attached to it, so successfully that the General could not observe it.'

What lessons were learnt about trench building?
Surprisingly quickly the Allies improved the quality of their trenches. No longer were they merely a jumping off point from which to launch an attack, but were designed and built to withstand an attack with overhead protection and the ability to see over, or through, the parapet in safety.

On 5 December 1914 Morgan Crofton wrote:

'An engineer officer is coming on Monday to instruct us in the art of building an "ideal trench". Instruction that is badly needed.'

On 7 December 1914 on visiting the 16th Infantry Brigade at trenches near La Bassée,

'They were dug in clumps large enough to hold three men each, each of these clumps were connected by a short communication trench to a long lateral trench which ran behind. This in turn was connected at intervals by trenches leading to dugouts where the men could rest when not actually using the front line. These dugouts were very comfortable, and lined with straw, and in the centre were braziers of coke or charcoal … All the trenches were connected up by telephones and the men received their food properly cooked and all their mail very frequently. The arrangements in rear of the trenches for lavatories were most elaborate … A system of mirrors rather like the periscope of a submarine allows the front to be watched without a man's head showing to be sniped at.'

A far cry from Zandvoorde only five weeks before!

A lack of appreciation by senior officers of the realities of trench warfare did persist though. On the last day of 1914 Morgan Crofton wrote,

> 'Brigade Headquarters today sent round to know "if, in the event of our returning to the trenches, it is considered necessary that the men should be equipped with entrenching tools". We do consider it necessary, but we sincerely trust that we shall not be wanted for such work.'

Headquarters were displaying a lack of appreciation of an entrenching tool's use in improving the trench, rescuing buried comrades following a collapse and as a close quarter weapon. It also shows wishful thinking on the part of the cavalry that their proto-infantry days were over and they could return to mounted warfare.

What lessons were learnt about infantry weapons?

Simply having rifles, bayonets and a couple of Maxim machine-guns was inadequate for infantry warfare.

The array of arms issued to the soldiers in 1918 was more comprehensive than those from 1914. Lightweight Lewis machine guns, hand grenades (Mills' Bombs) and trench mortars were just some of the weapons the infantry could use to attack and defend themselves.

As early as January 1915 soldiers were taught to use rudimentary hand grenades,

> 'We received orders today to send all officers into Hazebrouck on Monday next to learn how to thrown hand grenades and bombs. This is most necessary, for no one here has the remotest idea of how to use these things. It will be a case of save me from my friends, when we get into the trenches again.'

The hand grenades were frighteningly primitive and demonstrated the urgency to bring in additional infantry weapons even if they were not fully developed.

What lessons were learnt about artillery defensive fire?
When a hostile infantry attack was being launched it should have been immediately stopped by a concentration of artillery, machine-gun and rifle fire as the enemy was seen leaving his front trenches.

Lord Hugh's comments about the lack of artillery support had already been made. The fact that Lord Hugh made use of soldiers as messengers, 'runners', was indicative that he had no better means of communication, i.e. a field telephone connected rearwards with a landline. Had there been communications that were still effective after the bombardment he could have called upon artillery support. This presupposes that the guns were available and ready for action. Later in the war artillery batteries would have already selected locations to bombard such as the enemy front line trenches and gaps in the wire in no man's land as defensive fire missions.

Lessons about the positioning of fire-trenches, artillery-proof overhead protection, effective machine-gun positioning, and defensive artillery fire missions were learnt as the war slowly ground on. Reviewing the bitter experiences of Zandvoorde and similar actions allowed the British Army to develop out of all recognition between 1914 and 1918.

In Memoriam

The noble sacrifice of Lord Hugh remains recognized and commemorated in England and Belgium.

Westminster Abbey Memorial Service
On Wednesday 2 April 1919 a service of remembrance was held in Westminster Abbey, London, in the presence of King George V, 'In memory of the Officers, Warrant Officers, Non-Commissioned Officers and Men of the Household Cavalry who have died whilst serving with their Regiments or other formations during the War, 1914–1918'.

The order of service started with verses from Ecclesiasticus (xliv, verses 13 & 14): 'Their glory shall not be blotted out and their name liveth to all generations.' The Regimental bands of 1/LG, 2/LG and RHG played the Eton Memorial March, 'Angelus' from 'Scene Pittoresques' by Massenet, 'When I am laid in Earth' by Purcell, 'Thou art passing hence' by Sullivan and Suite from 'Les Erinnyes' by Massenet.

The Dean of Westminster Abbey's prayer included:

'They were men who endured hardships with patience, and faced dangers with cheerfulness. They fought valiantly and well. They gave themselves, they gave their all, the promise of their manhood, the flower of their strength. Through them has been won the great victory; through them we stand at the gateway of Peace, through them has been obtained the assurance of Freedom. Theirs has been the great sacrifice; and we thank God it has not been made in vain.'

Household Cavalry Memorial
The RHG machine-gun section attached to Lord Hugh's squadron was commanded by Lord Charles Sackvile Pelham Worsley. His burial spot was

The Household Cavalry Memorial in Zandvoorde. (*M. J. McBride*)

'Looking south.' One cross has Lord Worsley RHG and the other 'GRAVE NOT TO BE TOUCHED'. (*Private Collection*)

discovered at Zandvoorde and although his body was later exhumed the spot where he was buried was chosen to build the Household Cavalry Memorial.

At 11.00 hours on 4 May 1924 Field Marshal Lord Douglas Haig unveiled the Household Cavalry memorial in Zandvoorde. The ceremony was attended by about 60 relatives including Lord Hugh's mother, the Dowager Duchess of Westminster.

Lord Haig's short speech said how proud he was to have been chosen by the King to represent him at this moving ceremony and to render to the memory of the heroes of the Household Cavalry the homage which their glorious sacrifice deserved. He went on

'They watered the fields of Flanders with their blood. They were wiped out in order to defend Zandvoorde at the moment when the enemy was attempting to break the British front, and contributed by their courage to the operation which took place on the Marne in those agonising days at the beginning of the war. They died for their country and for the cause of freedom, and in doing so gained the right to eternal gratitude. They sleep in the fraternal soil on which they fought with their French and Belgian comrades.'

The Household Cavalry Memorial has the following inscription:

'To those of the 1st and 2nd Life Guards and Royal Horse Guards who died fighting in France & Flanders 1914. Many of them fell in defence of the ridge upon which this cross stands.'

The Memorial honours the following soldiers,

1st Life Guards
Lieutenant Colonel EB Cook MVO
Major Lord John Cavendish DSO
Capytain EDF Kelly, Captain Hon. WR Wyndham, Captain JF Todd (30th CIH), Captain Lord Hugh Grosvenor
Lt ALE Smith MC, Lt HAB St. George, Lt Hon G Ward, Lt JASC Anstruther (6 Dragoons), Lt JC Close Brooks, Lt Sir R Levinge Bt

Household Cavalry Memorial, Zandvoorde. (*Wayne Evans*)

Household Cavalry Memorial, Zandvoorde. (*Wayne Evans*)

SS JT Webb

CoH A Rose, CoH CL Holmes, CoH H Colclough (6 Dragoons), CoH HW Dawes, CoH J Arthur, CoH JW Wise, CoH P Bruce, CoH W Middleton (3 Dragoons), CoH WT Leggett

Cpl C Adams, Cpl CE Moulson (14 Lancers), Cpl E Fraser (3 Dragoons), Cpl FW Moore, Cpl H Turner (1st (Kings) DGs), Cpl J Kirkpatrick (1st (Kings) DGs), Cpl JH Critchley (1st (Kings) DGs), Cpl T Pate, Cpl TG Neighbour, Cpl W Oliver (1 Dragoons), Cpl W Rhodes, Cpl WJ Mews (16 Lancers)

LCpl E Blackwell (17 Lancers), LCpl E Maidment (5 Dragoons)

Tpr A Burrows, Tpr A Davies (6 Dragoons), Tpr A Richardson (1st Dragoons), Tpr A Stone, Tpr AH Farmer, Tpr AH Taylor (1st (Kings) DGs), Tpr AJ Blackmore, Tpr AJ Ford, Tpr AJ Gray (5 Dragoons), Tpr B Reddington, Tpr C Allison (17 Lancers), Tpr C Pickett (6 Dragoons), Tpr CCV Green (6 Dragoons), Tpr CH Cunningham (1st (Kings) DGs), Tpr CR Spoor, Tpr CW Child, Tpr D Barwell (3 Dragoons), Tpr DC Stewart, Tpr E Anderson (6 Dragoons), Tpr E Carver (16 Lancers), Tpr E Etchells (6 Dragoons), Tpr E Lewry, Tpr E Woolward (7 Dragoons), Tpr EA Buckley (3 Dragoons), Tpr EA Phillip (6 Dragoons), Tpr EE Hopkins (5 Dragoons), Tpr EL Lawson, Tpr F Bates (6 Dragoons), Tpr F Paget, Tpr F Richards (1st Dragoons), Tpr FJ Hudson, Tpr FM Burnett (1st Dragoons), Tpr FS Rogers, Tpr FS Rose (1st (Kings) DGs), Tpr FS Tingley, Tpr G Bugler (11 Hussars), Tpr G Marsh, Tpr GE Whitehead, Tpr GH Hopkins, Tpr GT Ingram, Tpr H Campbell, Tpr H Cootes (6 Dragoons), Tpr H Hickling, Tpr H Lord, Tpr H McDermott (1st (Kings) DGs), Tpr H Savage, Tpr H Streeter, Tpr HW Batchelor (3 Dragoons), Tpr I McMullan, Tpr J Batchelor (3 Dragoons), Tpr J Berry, Tpr J Black, Tpr J Dix, Tpr J George, Tpr J Hamilton (6 Dragoons), Tpr J Morley, Tpr J Ordway (3 Dragoons), Tpr J Pike (1st (Kings) DGs), Tpr J Proburte, Tpr J Randall (5 Dragoons), Tpr J Robinson, Tpr J Scothern, Tpr J Wood, Tpr JH Boddie (1st Dragoons), Tpr JJ White, Tpr JW Backhurst (6 Dragoons), Tpr JW Bryant (17 Lancers), Tpr LS Burrington, Tpr M Line (1st (Kings) DGs), Tpr OC Simms, Tpr OJ Archer (17 Lancers), Tpr R Buckett (5 Dragoons), Tpr R Keogh, Tpr R Peverill, Tpr R Smart (3

Dragoons), Tpr RAS Beck (11 Hussars), Tpr S Skelly (6 Dragoons), Tpr SE Sollars, Tpr SH Browne, Tpr SJ Browne, Tpr T King (2nd Dragoons), Tpr T Naismith (6 Dragoons), Tpr TH Brooms, Tpr TH Helllwell, Tpr V Dennee, Tpr W Black (6 Dragoons), Tpr W Bolton (5 Dragoons), Tpr W Bow (6 Dragoons), Tpr W Brandram (17 Lancers), Tpr W Buckeridge (6th Inniskilling Dragoons), Tpr W Cameron (6 Dragoons), Tpr W Dykes (6 Dragoons), Tpr W Grier, Tpr W Miller (6 Dragoons), Tpr W Woodward, Tpr WA Bishop, Tpr WA Buffham (2nd Dragoons), Tpr WE Gladman, Tpr WE Lane, Tpr WG Burgess (3 Dragoons), Tpr WG Levy, Tpr WH Lush, Tpr WS Adams (17 Lancers)

2nd Life Guards

Major Hon H Dawnay DSO

Capt AM Vandaleur, Capt FPC Pemberton, Capt Hon A O'Neill

Lt AG Murray Smith, Lt Sir RGV Duff Bt

2nd Lt WS Peterson

CoH A Ellison, CoH AH Backhouse, CoH C Coxhead, CoH C Wells, CoH H Piggott (13 Hussars), CoH RA More, CoH WC Stevenson

Cpl A Bullivant, Cpl ACN Dean, Cpl HA Payne, Cpl MG Taylor, Cpl P Forde

LCpl A Healey (10 Hussars), LCpl W Broom (14 Hussars), LCpl WH Owen (14 Hussars)

Tpr A Jones (17 Lancers), Tpr A Wackett, Tpr A Wardle (16 Lancers), Tpr AC Murray (6 Dragoons), Tpr AE De Laine, Tpr AE Seymour, Tpr AF Taunt (14 Hussars), Tpr Af Watkin, Tpr AG Hagues, Tpr AH Scott, Tpr AH White (3 Dragoons), Tpr AY Hutchison (11 Huteare), Tpr BJ Jones (3 Dragoons), Tpr C King, Tpr CR Goulding, Tpr D Black, Tpr D Hillier (13 Hussars), Tpr D Mclaren (17 Lancers), Tpr D Strachan (3 Dragoons), Tpr DF Sherlock, Tpr E Cooper, Tpr E Jones (20 Hussars), Tpr E Pacey (3 Dragoons), Tpr E Richardson (8 Hussars), Tpr E Smith (13 Hussars), Tpr E Tyrell (14 Hussars), Tpr EH Owens, Tpr F Jenkins, Tpr F McKellar, Tpr F Robinson (17 Lancers), Tpr F Sainsbury, Tpr F Smith (20 Hussars), Tpr F Stephenson (17

Lancers), Tpr F Wagstaffe (17 Lancers), Tpr FC Keene, Tpr FC Wickson (3 Dragoons), Tpr FE Mills, Tpr FS Whitbread (17 Lancers), Tpr G Foster (20 Hussars), Tpr GE Meyer, Tpr GJ Potter, Tpr GN Hawkes, Tpr GS Hadwen (6 Dragoons), Tpr H Davis, Tpr H Haines (13 Hussars), Tpr H Hellett (20 Hussars), Tpr H Higgleton (20 Hussars), Tpr HA Hastings, Tpr HB Molyneux, Tpr HG Boyce, Tpr HJF White (3 Dragoons), Tpr HS Wassmer (17 Lancers), Tpr HW Strutt (14 Hussars), Tpr J Bryce, Tpr J Hail (14 Hussars), Tpr J Hodgins, Tpr J McCombe (13 Hussars), Tpr J Mead (16 Lancers), Tpr J Seville (17 Lancers), Tpr J Squire, Tpr J Stevenson (14 Hussars), Tpr J Walker (11 Hussars), Tpr J Watson (8 Hussars), Tpr JA Pettigrew (17 Lancers), Tpr LJ Brooke (14 Hussars), Tpr MH Rouse, Tpr P McDermott (6 Dragoons), Tpr P Pickavance (14 Hussars), Tpr P Rafferty (17 Lancers), Tpr P Sullivan (3 Dragoons), Tpr R Grainger (20 Hussars), Tpr R Smith, Tpr S Garty (20 Hussars), Tpr S Oatley, Tpr SG Mudd (17 Lancers), Tpr SJ Randall, Tpr SJ Stevens, Tpr T Barlow (20 Hussars), Tpr T McVay (20 Hussars), Tpr TC Lloyd, Tpr W Hawkins, Tpr W Hawksworth (20 Hussars), Tpr W Kitchen, Tpr W McAulay (13 Hussars), Tpr W Neild (17 Lancers), Tpr W Sloan, Tpr WC Herring, Tpr WC Perry, Tpr WJ Westbrook (17 Lancers), Tpr WP Gamage (13 Hussars), Tpr WV Stewart (3 Dragoons)

Royal Horse Guards

Lt Col GC Wilson MVO

Major Viscount Crichton MVO DSO

Lt Baron A De Gunsberg, Lt GV Naylor Leyland, Lt PV Heath, Lt Lord Worsley

2nd Lt Hon F Lambton

CoH W Cole, CoH WG Ervin, CoH AG Few, CoH JC Harris

Cpl M Browning, Cpl WA Claybyn, Cpl SST Coles, Cpl CH White

LCpl FH Burfield, LCpl FH Harper

Tpr H Weaver (13 Hussars), Tpr J Wright (8 Hussars), Tpr L Wright (10 Hussars), Tpr A Cochrane, Tpr A Rathmell, Tpr G Chapman

(17 Lancers), Tpr J Clark (17 Lancers), Tpr J Cox (17 Lancers), Tpr A Crow (16 Lancers), Tpr T Davies (17 Lancers), Tpr J Davison (5 Lancers), Tpr TR Dawes (3 Dragoons), Tpr E Deverill (17 Lancers), Tpr R Dockeray (17 Lancers), Tpr FG Ernescliffe (11 Hussars), Tpr J Fisher (6 Dragoons), Tpr R Foreman (5 Lancers), Tpr CW Greiner (16 Lancers), Tpr C Hanna (6 Dragoons), Tpr A Hewitt (17 Lancers), Tpr B Hughes (17 Lancers), Tpr J Jaqueman (3 Dragoons), Tpr AA Jordan (16 Lancers), Tpr AA Kingswell (17 Lancers), Tpr GE Lea (17 Lancers), Tpr G Mason (17 Lancers)

In October 1924 Lord Worsley's father, the 4th Earl of Yarborough, wrote:

'From the sea to the Somme the path can be marked by the graves of the Household Cavalry, but in history, Zandvoorde may well stand as the scene in which these troops rendered their noblest and costliest contribution to the Allied cause. One can hardly conceive a more fitting memorial to the Household Cavalry than its present site, for it was upon the Zandvoorde Ridge that at the close of October 1914, the three regiments fought one of their most desperate actions and sustained, perhaps, their greatest losses in the War. The fact that the list of names reaches from top to bottom of the lofty shaft is proof of the toll taken of those famous regiments, when after three days and nights of incessant bombardment from three sides, culminating in an inferno of shell-fire, which obliterated the so-called trenches, and an overwhelming attack by the German XV Army Corps, the remnants of the Brigade were forced back upon their scanty reserves and the most exposed salient then in the Ypres defences passed into German hands. The First and Second Life Guards each lost a complete squadron and the Royal Horse Guards, as has been related, their Machine Gun section under Worsley. The presence of this splendid monument on the historic ridge will surely be a perpetual consolation to the relatives of those whose names are inscribed on it and the thought that the arduous days of ten years ago are thus commemorated, will no doubt be ever an inspiration to the splendid regiments of the Household Cavalry for many years to come.'

Ypres (Menin Gate) Memorial

In the immediate aftermath of the First World War there was a movement in Britain and Canada for Ypres to be preserved. Winston Churchill addressed the Imperial War Graves Commission London 21 January 1919,

> 'I should like us to acquire the whole of the ruins of Ypres … A more sacred place for the British race does not exist in the world.'

However, it was decided to rebuild Ypres and the memorial was to focus on the Menin Gate.

In July 1927 Sir Hubert Plumer (commander of the British 2nd Army) opened the Menin Gate in Ypres memorial to the missing. 'He is not missing.

Ypres (Menin Gate) Memorial. (*Wayne Evans*)

He is here'. The site of the Menin Gate was chosen because of the hundreds of thousands of men who passed through it on their way to the battlefields. It commemorates casualties from the forces of Australia, Canada, India, South Africa and United Kingdom who died in the Salient. The YPRES (MENIN GATE) MEMORIAL now bears the names of more than 54,000 officers and men whose graves are not known. The memorial was designed by Sir Reginald Blomfield with sculpture by Sir William Reid-Dick. Each evening since 1 May 1929 (apart from 1940 to 1944) the last post has been sounded by the local Fire Service.

Additionally 35,000 British and New Zealand servicemen who were killed after 16 August 1917 are commemorated on the Tyne Cot Memorial near Paschendeale. Inscribed on the Menin Gate are the Latin words taken from

Captain Lord Hugh Grosvenor's name and 54,000 others who are missing have their names carved with pride on the Ypres Memorial – the Menin Gate. (*Wayne Evans*)

an ode by Horace 'Dulce et decorum est pro patria mori', translated as 'it is sweet and fitting to die for one's country'. In a counterpoint to this sentiment is the poem by Wilfred Owen 'Dulce et Decorum Est' which ends with these lines, 'The old Lie; Dulce et Decorum est pro patria mori.'

Lord Hugh's name is inscribed on Panel 3 of the Menin Gate and the Grave Registration Report reads follows:

> 'GROSVENOR, Capt. Lord Hugh William. 1st Life Guards. Killed in action 30th Oct., 1914. Age 30. Son of the 1st Duke of Westminster and Katharine Duchess of Westminster; husband of Lady Hugh Grosvenor (now Lady Mabel Hamilton-Stubber), of 9, Southwick Crescent, London.'

Zantvoort (sic) British Cemetery

The Commonwealth War Graves Commission (CWGC) maintain a cemetery on Kruisekestraat, Zandvoorde.

The ethos of the then Imperial War Graves Commission (now the CWGC) was that the bodies of soldiers who died in battle during the First World War would not be repatriated home but interred near to where they fell.

Large cemeteries had a stone Cross of Sacrifice installed. Each headstone would be similar in Portland stone bearing the cap badge and details of the soldier, where known. Relatives could add an inscription at their own cost. The design of each of the Commonwealth War Graves cemeteries is unique. Sometimes roses are planted on every other grave so in theory the shadow of an English rose would fall on every headstone every day. Each cemetery will have a cabinet containing a visitor book.

An interpretation board stands outside Zantvoorde British Cemetery with the following inscription:

> 'Designed by noted architect Charles Holden, Zantvoorde British Cemetery was formed after the Armistice when Commonwealth burials were concentrated here from the nearby battlefields and from German cemeteries. There are now more than 1,580 servicemen of the First World War buried or commemorated in the cemetery, most of whom remain unidentified. Of those whose names are known, over a

Zantvoorde British Military Cemetery with the Cross of Sacrifice in the background. (*M. J. McBride*)

quarter died in the desperate fighting of October and November 1914 around Zantvoorde (now Zandvoorde), Zillebeck and Gheluvelt as Allied troops strove to prevent the German forces from seizing the high ground overlooking Ypres and reaching the Channel ports.

'The Fall of Zantvoorde Village, October 1914
'Units of the British Expeditionary Force (BEF) first clashed with the German Army in this sector on 19 October 1914 as they moved toward Menin and encountered German forces advancing from the other direction in an attempt to take Ypres. Heavy fighting to the north and south of the Menin Road saw the front-line move back and forth over the next three weeks as British and French forces tried to stop the German advance as far away from Ypres as possible.

'By 30 October the officers and men of the elite Household Cavalry had positioned themselves in shallow, improvised trenches just east of the village. The cavalrymen in front of Zantvoorde should have been relieved the night before and sent to the rear for a much-needed rest,

One of many headstones
in Zantvoorde cemetery of
unidentified soldiers 'Known
Unto God'. (*M. J. McBride*)

but enemy pressure in the sector was so great that their relief was sent
to support another part of the line. These units of Life Guards and
Royal Horse Guards had been ordered to dismount and defend the
British front-line using every man who could fire a rifle, including
those usually assigned to transport and other non-combatant duties.
Only a very small number of units were held in reserve for deployment
to sections of the line that were in imminent danger of breaking.

'At 6.45 on this dull, misty morning, artillery fire began to rain down
on the British positions. For more than an hour it seemed as if every
one of the 260 German heavy guns in the sector were concentrated on
the scant lines of cavalry and men were killed, wounded, and buried as
their trenches were blown in. Those who survived the bombardment
then faced an infantry attack of overwhelming force at 8 am. In the
1st Life Guards alone more than five officers and 100 men were killed

or missing by 10 am, one Squadron losing all but one man, who was badly shaken by his experiences. Despite this determined defence of the village, the Germans soon took Zantvoorde and the troops of the cavalry brigade were forced back to a new line in front of the village of Klein Zillebeke. German gunners immediately took advantage of their newly gained high ground to fire shells into the British lines east and west of Zantvoorde. Counter-attacks were mounted to retake the village but failed in the face of heavy artillery fire and large numbers of fresh German troops. The village had been captured and would remain in German hands until 28 September 1918.

'The chaotic nature of the fighting that took place around Zantvoorde in October 1914 is revealed by the number of men who were killed in action but have no known grave. Many of those who fell while attempting to defend the village were subsequently buried by the Germans as unidentified British soldiers and today are either commemorated on the Menin Gate or lie beneath headstones that bear Rudyard Kipling's immortal words, 'Known Unto God'.'

Zandvoorde Willow, Combermere Barracks, Windsor
The plaque is inscribed:

'This willow tree was presented in 1963 by Colonel Gerald Grosvenor in memory of his father, Captain Lord Hugh Grosvenor, 1st Life Guards who was killed in action at Zandvoorde on the 30th October 1914. This tree is a descendant of a cutting taken in 1918 from the shattered willow stump that was the only living thing in an area of complete devastation and was growing on a position held by C Squadron 1st Life Guards 29th to 30th October 1914.'

This Willow tree was grown from a cutting recovered from Zandvoorde at the end of the First World War. (*M. J. McBride*)

St John's Hyde Park, London
Lord Hugh's name is inscribed on the cross outside St John's Church and
on the plaque inside.

St John's Church, Hyde Park Crescent, London. The Celtic cross is on the left. (*M. J. McBride*)

Across the road from Lord and Lady Grosvenor's home on Southwick (now Hyde Park) Crescent is St John's Church. A Celtic style of cross stands outside in memory of soldiers from the parish who

'To the glory of God and in grateful memory of the men who by God's grace victorious fought for their country and died that the cause of freedom and right might triumph and more particularly of the men of this parish whose names are inscribed hereunder 'Death is swallowed up in victory'

Inside St John's church a brass plaque is displayed with the same wording as that used on the cross outside. (*M. J. McBride*)

St Mary's Church, Eccleston, Chester

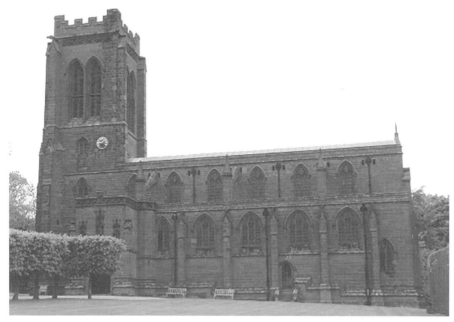

St Mary's Church, Eccleston, Chester. (*M. J. McBride*)

Bronze relief of Lord Hugh in St Mary's Church, Eccleston, Chester. (*M. J. McBride*)

The inscription underneath:

To the Glory of God
In proud and grateful memory of
Hugh William Grosvenor
Captain and Commanding C Squadron
of the 1st Regiment of Life Guards
son of
Hugh Lupus 1st Duke of Westminster
and Katherine his wife
He gave his life for his country at Zandvoorde
during the First Battle of Ypres
on the 30th Day of October 1914
Aged 30

Eaton Estate, Chester

Painting of Captain Lord Hugh William Grosvenor in Eaton Hall, Chester. (*Private collection*)

Captain Lord Hugh William Grosvenor's medals with the oak leaf sewn onto the medal ribbon indicating Mention in Despatches. The three medals were commonly referred to as Pip, Squeak and Wilfred.

The Death Memorial Plaque for Captain Lord Hugh William Grosvenor.

HE whom this scroll commemorates was numbered among those who at the call of King and Country, left all that was dear to them, endured hardness, faced danger, and finally passed out of the sight of men by the path of duty and self-sacrifice, giving up their own lives that others might live in freedom. Let those who come after see to it that his name be not forgotten.

Capt. Lord Hugh William Grosvenor
1st Life Guards
October 30. 1914.

Memorial scroll dedicated to Captain the Lord Hugh William Grosvenor. This scroll was given to his next-of-kin along with a Memorial Death Plaque. This was more commonly referred to as the Dead Man's Penny. The issuing of the plaque started in 1916 with the realization by the British Government that some form of official token of gratitude should be given to the fallen service men and women's bereaved next of kin.

The plaque is a 12 centimetre disc cast in bronze gunmetal, which incorporated the following: an image of Britannia and a lion, two dolphins representing Britain's sea power, and the emblem of Imperial Germany's eagle being torn to pieces by another lion. Britannia is holding an oak spray with leaves and acorns. Beneath this was a rectangular tablet where the deceased individual's name was cast into the plaque. No rank was given as it was intended to show equality in their sacrifice. On the outer edge of the disc were the words 'He died for freedom and honour'.

Bibliography

1914–18 3rd Cavalry Division, 7th Cavalry Brigade, 1st Life Guards Oct 1914 – Mar 1918 (National Archives WO 95/1155/1)

2nd Life Guards WW1 War Diaries (The National Archives WO95/1155 and 1135)

Ali, Jonathan. *Our Boys. The Great War in a Lancashire Village* (Landy Publishing 2007)

Anglesey, Marquess of. *History of the British Cavalry* (Leo Cooper, London 1997)

Badsey, Stephen. *Doctrine and Reform in the British Cavalry 1880–1918* (Ashgate, Aldershot 2008)

Bessemer, Paul. *In memory of Lieutenant Charles Sackville Pelham, Lord Worsley* (Unpublished. 2016)

Bingham, Lt-Col R.C. *Squadron of the Lost* (Sunday Graphic and Sunday News 1933)

Binks, Steve. *Battlefield Notes* (2011)

Bird, Antony. *Gentlemen, we will stand and fight* (Cromwell Press 2008)

Cornish, Paul. *Machine-guns and The Great War* (Pen & Sword 2009)

Cox & Co, *List of British Officers taken prisoner in the various Theatres of War between August 1914 and November 1918* (London 1919)

Cornwell, Bernard. *Waterloo* (William Collins 2014)

Crookenden, Colonel Arthur. *History of the Cheshire Regiment in the Great War* (The Naval and Military Press 2009)

Decuypere, Dirk. *Het Melheur Van De Keizer – 1914–1918* (1998)

Douglas Haig War Diaries and Letters 1914–18, Gary Sheffield and John Bourne, 2005, BCA

Edmonds, Brigadier General Sir James. *History of the Great War, Military Operations France & Belgium 1914* (Imperial War Museum 1925)

Evans, Martin Marix. *Battles of WWI* (Arcturus 2008)

Farrar-Hockley, General Sir Anthony. *Ypres. Death of an Army.* (Arthur Barker Ltd 1967)

Field, Leslie. *Bendor. The Golden Duke of Westminster* (Weidenfeld and Nicolson 1983)

Gall, H.R. *Modern Tactics* (London, W.H. Allen 1890)

Gardiner, Ian. *The Flatpack Bombers, The Royal Navy and The Zeppelin Menace* (Pen & Sword Publishing Ltd 2009)

Gaskill, Matthew. *The German Army and Stormtroops of World War One* (2014)

Gleichen, Edward. *Infantry Brigade 1914* (Leonaur Ltd 2007)

Gliddon, Gerald. *The Aristocracy and the Great War* (2002 Norwich)

Hamilton, Captain Lord Ernest William. *The First Seven Divisions, Being a detailed account of the fighting from Mons to Ypres* (Pickle Partners Publishing 1916)

Holmes, Richard. *Riding the Retreat Mons to Marne 1914 revisited* (Pimlico 1995)

Hyndson, J.G.W., M.C., *From Mons to the First Battle of Ypres* (Wyman 1932)

Infantry Training, (War Office 1914)

Jünger, Ernst. *Storm of Steel* (The Penguin Press 1920)

Kenyon, David. *Horsemen in No Man's Land, British Cavalry and Trench Warfare* 1914–18 (Pen & Sword 2011)

Lloyd, R.A. *A trooper in the 'Tins' – Autobiography of a Lifeguardsman* (Hurst & Blackett London 1938)

Lomas, David. *Mons 1914* (Osprey 1997)

Macdonald, Lyn. *1914 Days of Hope* (Penguin Books 1987)

Martin. *Cavalry of the Great War*

Murland, Jerry. *Aristocrats Go To War* (Pen & Sword 2010)

Neillands, Robin. *The Old Contemptibles: The British Expeditionary Force 1914,*

Notes for Infantry Officers on Trench Warfare (War Office 1916)

Notes from the Front, Part 1, Tactical Notes, (1914)

Olsen, Richard. *An Inspirational Warrior: Major General Sir Thompson Capper*

Oliver, Michael and Partridge, Richard. *The Battle of Albuera 1811 'Glorious Field of Grief'* (Pen & Sword 2007)

Pegler, Martin. *Sniping in the Great War.* (2008, Barnsley)

Ramsbottom, Roy F. *Marching as to War,*

Rogers, Major Brian. *Zandvoorde.* (Household Cavalry Journal 2014)

Roynon, Gavin, *Massacre of the Innocents, The Crofton Diaries YPRES 1914–15* (Stroud, 2004)

Jones, Spencer. *Scouting for Soldiers: Reconnaissance and the British Cavalry 1899–1914* (Sage Publications 2011)

Sheldon, Jack. *The German Army at Ypres 1914* (Pen & Sword 2010)

Spagnoly, Tony and Smith, Ted. *Cameos of the Western Front: Salient Points Two Ypres Sector 1914–18* (Leo Cooper / Pen & Sword 1998)

Strachan, Hew. *The Oxford Illustrated History of the First World War* (Oxford 1998)

Sykes, Lieutenant-Colonel. *Transfer Memorandum 1st August 1913* (The National Archives WO339/9147 C674737)

Wainwright, John. *First World War interview 10600* (Imperial War Museum 1988)

War Diary of the 1st Life Guards

Westminster Abbey memorial service for members of the Household Cavalry who died during the War 1914–1918

Ypres 1914 an official account published by order of the German General Staff (1917)

Index